WAGES, RACE, SKILLS AND SPACE

CONTEMPORARY URBAN AFFAIRS
VOLUME 5
GARLAND REFERENCE LIBRARY OF SOCIAL SCIENCE
VOLUME 1170

CONTEMPORARY URBAN AFFAIRS
RICHARD D. BINGHAM, *Series Editor*

Wages, Race, Skills and Space

Lessons from Employers in Detroit's Auto Industry

Susan Turner Meiklejohn

The Maxine Goodman Levin College of Urban Affairs at Cleveland State University

Garland Publishing, Inc.
a member of the Taylor & Francis Group
New York & London
2000

Published in 2000 by
Garland Publishing, Inc.
A member of the Taylor & Francis Group
29 West 35th Street
New York, NY 10001

10   9   8   7   6   5   4   3   2   1

Library of Congress Cataloging-in-Publication Data

Meiklejohn, Susan Turner.
    Wages, race, skills and space : lessons from employers in Detroit's auto
industry / Susan Turner Meiklejohn.
        p. cm — (Garland reference library of social sciences ; v. 1170. Con-
temporary urban affairs ; v. 5)
    Includes bibliographical references and index.
    ISBN 0-8153-2844-3 (alk. paper)
    1. Discrimination in employment—Michigan—Detroit. 2. Afro-Ameri-
can automobile industry workers—Michigan—Detroit. I. Title. II. Garland
reference library of social science; v. 1170. III. Garland reference library of
social science. Contemporary urban affiars; v. 5.

HD4903.3.A82 U65 2000
331.6'396073077434–dc21   99-051638

Printed on acid-free, 250-year-life paper
Manufactured in the United States of America

For my guys
Alec Meiklejohn and Emile Haynie
who bring me such comfort and joy

Contents

Series Editor's Foreword

Susan Turner Meiklejohn's *Wages, Race, Skills and Space: Lessons from Employers in Detroit's Auto Industry* is an important study of wage and employment differences between blacks and whites in an urban economy. The book presents the results of a Detroit-based research endeavor which sought to understand the role of employer practices, geography, job skills, and the characteristics of workers in explaining economic disparities between black and white workers.

In this qualitative study, Meiklejohn designed a case-match format to be able to compare 13 black-owned firms and 13 white-owned firms. Firms were matched by technology used, location, size, and product produced. She conducted 52 interviews at these firms. The length of the interviews ranged from one to five hours with a mean of 90 minutes. Interviews were conducted with CEOs and with floor supervisors who had day-to-day contact with entry-level workers.

Meiklejohn finds that black employers are more likely to hire black workers, but both black and white employers with largely black workforces pay significantly lower wages than employers with largely white workforces. She also finds what appears to be discriminatory hiring practices in largely white suburban firms and harassment of black workers in the suburbs. However, the labor-force problems of blacks are complex. For example, it is extremely difficult for urban residents without cars to adequately search for higher-paying jobs in the suburbs—especially when employers recruit by posting signs in their windows or by word of mouth. Meiklejohn concludes with policy recommendations to reduce hiring discrimination.

Richard D. Bingham

Acknowledgments

Sheldon Danziger provided detailed and helpful comments to an earlier version of this book. John Nystuen, Mary Corcoran, and Reynolds Farley also provided excellent feedback on my first draft. Harry Holzer and Chris Tilly shared early versions of their work with me and they, along with Sanders Korenman, very much aided my understanding of the issues I address here.

Information from chapters 4 and 5 was previously published in a different form as "Barriers to a Better Break: Employer Discrimination and Spatial Mismatch in Metropolitan Detroit." *Journal of Urban Affairs 19,* 2 : 123–141.

List of Tables

Introduction

In the years between World War II and the 1960s, African Americans made considerable gains relative to whites in terms of labor-force participation, employment rates, occupational distribution in higher-paying jobs, and earnings (Jaynes and Williams, 1989). However, in the 1960s, this narrowing gap began to widen again as relative joblessness among blacks increased and continued to climb through the 1970s and 1980s. Earnings gaps between whites and blacks also sharply increased in the 1980s and early 1990s (Bound and Freeman, 1992; Corcoran and Parrott, 1992). Now, during the relatively strong economy of the late 1990s, employment gaps between blacks and whites are beginning to close again, but wage and income disparities persist.

The recent economic recovery has reduced unemployment for all groups. In 1998 the overall unemployment rate has been below 5 percent for the past year (Economic Report of the President [ERP], 1998), and reached the 27-year low of 4.3 percent in January 1999. However, substantial differences persist between black and white unemployment on a national level; the unemployment rate of 8.4 percent for black men is the lowest annual average since 1974, but it is well above the unemployment rate of 3.6 percent for white men. Labor-force participation for black men is 84 percent, compared to 93 percent for whites.[1]

Although labor-force participation for all women has increased in the last 20 years, the rates for black women exceeded those of whites, accelerating to 64 percent in 1997, compared to 60 percent for white women—the latter rate could be characterized as a plateau. However, black women also have higher unemployment rates than white women.

Median incomes are somewhat higher among blacks than they were 25 years ago, but the rising median income among blacks has not kept pace with the rising median income of whites. In 1998 the median income increased 14 percent for whites, but only 9 percent for blacks. More telling, when examining persistent economic gaps between blacks and whites, is the fact that the 1998 black median income was about 56 percent that of whites, a bigger gap than in 1972 (ERP, 1998). Although persistent joblessness and relatively low earnings are features of every age and education group of African Americans, black youth are particularly affected (Jencks and Mayer, 1989).

There is a significant body of recent writings where various explanations had been put forward for why these economic gaps between blacks and whites persist, and by some indicators, continue to grow.[2] These explanations loosely fall into three categories: space, skills, and race.

Most theorists addressing the worsening position of blacks in the labor market generally fall within the space and skills camps (and many note the interaction of the two). For example, the "spatial mismatch" theory emphasizes what many consider to be the negative effects of growing geographic distances between suburban jobs and largely urban minority populations. Spatial mismatch theorists also acknowledge what they consider to be perhaps a concomitant "skills mismatch": that the market is increasingly placing more emphasis on skills that minority workers may be deficient of in spite of recent educational gains, such as technical skills, or communication and interpersonal skills.

With a few notable exceptions, race-centered explanations, such as the growth or persistence of discriminatory employer attitudes and hiring practices, have received relatively little attention.[3] For example, William Julius Wilson has stressed that racial discrimination is a problem in terms of its *legacy* rather than its current actuality. Wilson writes that it is the historic barring of blacks from certain trades or sectors in the past that has impeded the formation of networks of friends and relatives who can smooth the way for a new crop of young workers into these areas.[4] He, along with many other authors who will be reviewed here, places far more emphasis on the skills, characteristics, and residential location of black workers than on the current attitudes and practices of employers.

This book describes findings from a Detroit-based research project I undertook in order to understand better the role of employer practices, along with space, the skill demands of jobs, and the characteristics of workers, in contributing to growing economic disparities between black and white workers.

I completed a qualitative study among a selected sample of employers in the auto-supply industry in the Detroit metropolitan area. I sought to evaluate the relative merit of space-, race-, and skill-based explanations for growing wage and employment gaps between relatively unskilled blacks and whites by interviewing employers using a case-match format that paired white-owned firms with black-owned firms on the basis of size, location, and product produced.[5] This format was used to separate out racial differences in employer attitudes and practices by contrasting the responses of employers from black- and white-owned firms.

A key finding from this study is the fact that black employers were more likely to hire black workers, but both black and white employers with largely black workforces pay significantly lower wages than employers with largely white workforces. This wage difference is the organizing element of chapters that address locational considerations, differences in recruitment and hiring practices among firms and possible differences in skill requirements among black- and white-owned firms, and/or differences in skill-related worker characteristics among employees. Woven into this story is evidence addressing continuing manifestation of employer racial discrimination.

The structure of this book, then, reflects the explanatory categories of space, skills, and race. I begin this discussion with a chapter that describes the rationale and methodology of the study. I follow this with an introductory "space" chapter that presents a brief history of spatial segregation in the Detroit metropolitan area; this chapter also includes a description the often contrasting characteristics of this city and its suburbs.

In chapter 3 I address another spatial aspect of employment before I begin my discussion of wages and space: I had asked black and white Detroit employers about their location and how they think customers and other outsiders view the city of Detroit. This discussion of the image of the city, as perceived by employers both in the cities and in the suburbs, may aid the understanding of findings presented in subsequent chapters. One interesting finding discussed in this chapter is that both black and white employers stated that the city of Detroit was perceived to be unsafe and threatening in the eyes of customers and other outsiders but that operating costs are cheaper there than in the surrounding suburbs. However, only black employers felt that the lower costs associated with a Detroit location, sometimes coupled with their community goals, outweighed the perceived costs of this city's negative image.

Chapter 4 details an unexpected research finding that pertains to wages and space. I found that the greater the proportion of black workers in a firm (regardless of the race of the owner), the lower the wages paid. White-owned suburban firms (hiring relatively few black workers) paid the highest wages of all. The key explanation for this appears to be that the boundaries of the city of Detroit define a labor market that has laws of supply and demand that are very different from those of the surrounding suburbs.

In chapter 5 I place these wage-related findings in the context of the spatial mismatch literature. I found that both black and white respondents described incidents of suburban harassment of blacks and recounted what appear to be discriminatory hiring practices on the part of white suburban employers: factors that may partially explain why more black urban residents do not seek better-paying suburban jobs. I also found that black-owned firms in the suburbs, and some white-owned suburban firms, have recruited a high number of minority workers. The white-owned organizations either chose or were forced to adhere to strict affirmative action guidelines. Therefore, spatial mismatch theory is presented with a twist: although the geographic inaccessibility of jobs is a problem for many urban residents, antidiscriminatory employer attitudes and practices may counter its effect.

Chapter 6 addresses skill issues and focuses on what some consider to be changing workplace skill demands and an inability of minority workers to keep up with these demands in spite of overall educational gains. While once the literature addressing skills focused on workers' "hard skills," such as reading, math, and measurement skills, there has been a new focus on what some scholars call "soft skills," such as work attitudes and interpersonal and communication skills. A key finding from the employer interviews completed as part of this study is that although black and white employers noted hard skill differences between black and white workers, they did not feel there were noticeable soft skill differences. In addition, the magnitude of perceived racially based hard skill differences, coupled with the demands of studied jobs, did not appear great enough to account for the stark wage difference between firms with majority-black and majority-white workforces.

Chapter 7 begins with a summary of current findings pertinent to discriminatory hiring and affirmative action and emphasizes my study findings pertinent to these issues. In the Detroit metropolitan area, suburban employment, particularly better-paying entry-level employment, is still largely off-limits to urban blacks, even if they had adequate transportation, while white employers are loath to locate in a majority-black city.

This book is written to stress that although it is essential to understand the relative importance of skill- and location-based explanations for continuing economic gaps between whites and blacks, it is equally important to consider that discriminatory employer attitudes and hiring practices may form as great a barrier to the acquisition of equal economic opportunity for minorities as relatively poor skills or restricted suburban housing opportunities. Therefore, it concludes with suggestions for needed actions to narrow wage and employment gaps between whites and blacks.

NOTES

[1] These percentages apply to men ages 25-64.

[2] Two relatively recent papers which summarize recent research exploring the various explanations for growing wage and employment gaps between blacks and whites: Moss and Tilly (1991a) and Holzer (1995).

[3] Kirschenman and Neckerman (1991), students of Wilson, provided a counterargument to him. Roger Waldinger also extensively addresses the role of discrimination in minority economic outcomes in his 1993 book *Still the Promised City?*

[4] This argument is most recently put forth in Wilson's book *When Work Disappears,* 1996.

[5] See note 1, above.

WAGES, RACE, SKILLS AND SPACE

CHAPTER 1

Study Rationale and Methodology

Three decades after the enactment of the 1964 Civil Rights Act, racial discrimination in both housing and employment continues to be a major problem in the United States.[1] As white urban residents and businesses continue to move away from most central cities, the majority of African Americans are still left behind in these areas to contend with the decline in services, decent housing, and educational and job opportunities that a steady outmigration of people and capital creates. Not only do these conditions negatively affect the employment chances of urban blacks but they also provide an additional impetus for the continued outmigration of residents and businesses (Holzer, 1991; Holzer, Ihlanfeldt, and Sjoquist, 1992).

The city of Detroit, long dependent on a single, cyclical industry, has suffered extensive capital disinvestment by businesses for nearly 50 years. The postwar suburban housing boom was accompanied by an extreme outmigration of population, jobs, and capital investment. The city's population fell from a high of nearly 1.85 million in 1952 to the 1990 count of just over one million, while surrounding suburban communities gained over a million new residents in the 20-year period from 1960 to 1980.

Between 1950 and 1990, Detroit's black population increased 159 percent, while the city's white population decreased by 86 percent. According to the 1990 census, 76 percent of the city's population is African American, while the surrounding suburban population is only 7 percent black. The Detroit metropolitan area is now the most racially segregated in the country; furthermore, segregation indices for the city and surrounding suburbs have not improved through the 1980s (Farley, Steeh and Krysan, 1994).

As a cause and consequence of this segregation, severe racial animosities persist in the Detroit area. Douglas Massey notes that the greater Detroit area is perhaps the best exemplar of spatial apartheid in the United States. Mike Davis emphasizes that Detroit competes with Atlanta for the distinction of being the most perfect "urban doughnut: black in the formerly industrialized center, lily-white in the job rich periphery" (Massey, 1990, and Davis, cited in Neill, 1995).

Growing geographic polarization between largely urban blacks and suburban whites may increase disparities between resources and opportunities for the two groups and reinforce cultural differences as well. The reduced probability of blacks and whites interacting on a day-to-day basis may increase the potential for stereotyping, and for employers to gain information from such sources as inflammatory media portrayals rather than firsthand experience.

Although the demographics of the Detroit area, with a population that is primarily black and non-Hispanic white, may not resemble those cities on the country's coasts that lend themselves to a more demanding analysis of how race and ethnicity plays out in the labor market, Detroit's relatively simple division of the population into black and white can perhaps allow a clearer and more straightforward insight into how employers view black workers.[2] There are far fewer groups, such as large new immigrant populations, contending for lower wages and lower-skilled jobs. If black workers are having more difficulty finding employment and earning a living wage in Detroit's metropolitan market than they had in the past, it can perhaps be assumed that the fate of lower-skilled African Americans is far worse in cities like Los Angeles and New York, where in-migration creates ever-increasing demand for available jobs.

By 1990, only 18 percent of jobs in the metropolitan area were located in the city of Detroit; the city suffered a 22 percent decline in the number of jobs from 1980 to 1990. The number of jobs in every job sector is decreasing in the city of Detroit—a pattern that differs from most other deindustrialized cities, where growth in service-sector jobs has offset declines in manufacturing. From the 1940s to the early 1980s, Detroit's share of the region's manufacturing employment fell from 60.3 to 25 percent. The city's retail share dropped from 72.6 to 15.4 percent, while services and wholesale trade shares fell from 75.3 to 23.6 percent, and from 90.1 to 29.6 percent respectively (Darden et al. 1987). The current economic and social ramifications of this out-migration of population and capital are extreme. In Detroit, black poverty increased from 26 to 38 percent of all households from 1980-1990; among whites it climbed from 6 to 8 percent (SEMCOG, 1994).

Other interrelated factors occurring on a national level that also manifest themselves in the Detroit metropolitan area and point to its appropriateness as a focus for this study include sectoral shifts and weakening antidiscrimination legislation. Targeted antidiscrimination legislation is applied only to those employers receiving government contracts. In the Detroit area, the employers who are required to enforce this legislation are primarily in government and manufacturing, two sectors that are rapidly declining (SEMCOG, 1994). At the same time, selective antidiscrimination sanctions, pertinent to other job sectors, have been legislatively weakened and have received a poor record of investigation during the Reagan-Bush years (Bendick, Jackson, and Reinaso, 1993).

Given these economic and social indicators, it is not surprising that Detroit has a high crime rate, although it is not as high as commonly perceived. In 1995, Detroit's crime rate ranked 23rd among cities with populations over one hundred thousand. By comparison, Fort Lauderdale, Florida, ranked 2nd for that year (Atlanta, Georgia was first), while Topeka, Kansas ranked 9th and Tucson, Arizona ranked 14th (Heinlein and Phillips, 1996). Detroit experienced a 12 percent drop in murders from 1994 to 1995 (murders were down 8 percent during this period for the nation as a whole.) Detroit burglaries fell over 4 percent between 1993 and 1994—beating the statewide average of a 3 percent drop (Heinlein, 1995). In addition, the city looks and feels abandoned; it isn't so much that homes, factories, and stores stand vacant (although many do), but that they no longer stand at all.[3] Large, unoccupied vistas now dominate the landscape; aerial photographs of Detroit show more green space than exists in much of the city's ex-urban fringe. Some argue that these areas are ripe for development, but, as former Detroit planning director Gloria Robinson has stressed, they are constrained by problems of uncertain ownership and environmental contamination (Robinson, 1994).

THE AUTO PARTS SUPPLY INDUSTRY IN THE CITY OF DETROIT

The unparalleled growth and decline of the auto industry laid the groundwork for the conditions—poverty, spatial isolation, and unemployment of black Detroiters—that are the focus of this study. The auto industry prompted the flow of both white people and jobs from the city center to the suburbs as early as the 1920s; even Henry Ford chose to base his home and part of his operations in the then-rural Dearborn in 1914.

This early, extensive, and rapid suburbanization was further encouraged by federal postwar housing and highway policies, and the availability of land. The auto industry was one of the powerful groups that lobbied the federal government to build the extensive and intricate highway system that simultaneously ruined city neighborhoods and created quick access (at least for white families) to the ever-growing suburbs.

Although the auto industry has recently faced massive losses, it still dominates the economic landscape in Detroit. Because of the crisis in the auto industry in the 1970s, Big Three automakers have implemented a variety of technical and organizational changes in an attempt to remain competitive; and such changes are also mandated for their suppliers. Moss and Tilly (1991b) found that more auto-related firms have implemented technological and organizational changes than any other studied firm type (including firms in the service sector).

The auto supply industry is a fertile case for examining changing skill needs. As Moss and Tilly noted in their work, CEOs and heads of personnel state that changes, such as the implementation of computerized numerical control machines and techniques like statistical process control, necessitate greater "hard" and "soft" skills, such as numeracy and teamwork. The auto-supply industry has also long employed black workers, at least as unskilled workers.[4]

The presence of blacks in many auto-supply firms may allow more realistic employer observations of young black workers. The same pressure from civil rights groups that forced the hiring of blacks in the industry is also the reason why there are more black owners of auto-supply companies than any other firm type in the Detroit area: the Big Three mandated the creation of black-owned supply firms.

However, I would like to note that through the course of my interviews, personnel managers and CEOs at 6 of the 13 "minority-owned" firms told me that their CEO was in partnership with a white co-owner. In the case of only one firm, Crowe Products Inc., the black owner seemed to have little say in firm decision-making.[5] Not surprisingly, this is the one black-owned firm whose hiring practices and racial representation among workers seemed more like white-owned suburban firms. In the other 5 cases of dual ownership, it appeared that the black owners had clear input into the management of the firm.[6]

Of the 13 black-owned firms, 4 had white floor supervisors (3 had a say in hiring). However, hiring at only one of these firms was solely conducted by a white person: this was at the suburban partially white-owned

Lionel Plastics, which had a 35 percent black workforce, one of the two lowest percentages of all black-owned firms. Therefore, with one exception, the hiring process was controlled by African Americans at the black-owned firms.

The result of this employer, personnel manager, and supervisor racial breakdown is as follows: I came away from my interviews with the heads of all the black firms with the view that they were committed to having a high percentage of entry-level black workers and were hiring relatively high numbers of minority workers.

RELATION OF THIS STUDY TO THE WORK OF OTHER SIMILAR RESEARCH PROJECTS

In 1987 and 1988, while at the University of Chicago, William Julius headed a research project called the "Urban Poverty and Family Life Study" (UPFLS). The UPFLS included several components, including a random survey of nearly twenty-five hundred residents of poor neighborhoods as well as a 1988 survey of 179 employers.[7] The format and preliminary results of the UPFLS provided a launching pad for a larger and more extensive research project designed to assess the relative importance of various explanations for growing gaps between minorities and whites: the Multi-City Survey of Urban Inequality (MCSUI), funded by the Ford, Russell Sage, and Rockefeller Foundations involved researchers from 17 universities who conducted household and employer surveys in four cities: Detroit, Los Angeles, Atlanta, and Boston.

From 1993 to 1995, I participated in the MCSUI, where in each city about two thousand household members were surveyed in their homes about their work histories and related issues. In addition, five hundred employers from each city were interviewed by telephone about the characteristics of the entry-level jobs they offer, their worker needs, and their hiring practices. Finally, in each city, representatives from 45 firms were statistically selected for face-to-face interviews from a larger sample. I conducted interviews with up to three respondents from half of the 45 Detroit firms.

Because of this selection process, no minority-owned firms, and few minority respondents, were included in the research process. To address this omission, I designed a survey-based qualitative research project that sought directly to compare the observations of employers and supervisors at black-owned firms with those at case-matched white-owned firms.

Like Wilson and MCSUI researchers, I was looking at three hypotheses for growing wage and employment disparities between blacks and whites. These were the notion of a spatial mismatch between black populations and available jobs, a perhaps concomitant skills mismatch between job demands and the attributes of workers, and negative employer attitudes toward black workers (particularly young, black males) that are reflected in discriminatory hiring practices.[8]

My case-match format was used to separate out racial differences in employer perceptions and practices by contrasting the responses of employers from the black-owned firms with those from case-matched white-owned firms.[9] I assumed that a black-white match would provide a control for discriminatory attitudes and practices among whites, as well as act as a mechanism to bring the perceptions and experiences of minority employers into a growing body of employer-based research.

SAMPLE SELECTION

I chose to interview automobile parts supply firms because they were the one specific firm type in Detroit that had at least 15 black owners. Black-owned businesses were identified through directories from the Detroit-area Minority Business Development Council, the State of Michigan Office of Civil Rights, a University of Michigan listing of minority business enterprises, and the privately owned Success Guide of Michigan. I initially identified 18 black-owned auto supply companies in the Detroit metropolitan area and then used a list of over 250 white-owned auto-supply companies obtained from Ford Motor Company to create matches of white-owned firms on the basis of size, location, and product production.

Number of Firms and Interviews

Out of the 18 identified black-owned firms, 4 were found to be either out of business or did not have a workforce of at least 6 people, the minimum size for this study. Out of 14 remaining eligible firms, only one refused to participate. Three of these firms were located in the suburbs.

After I obtained the permission of key personnel from the 13 black-owned firms, white-owned firms were selected to create the most exact match possible regarding location, size, and product lines. As can be seen in table 1-1, which presents information about participating firms, some cases do not have an exact locational match (by neighborhood) because there are so few white-owned firms in the city. With the exception of the Woodward/USG match, the firms are similar in terms of size and

Table 1-1 Firm Profiles

Firm	Year Found.	Firm Type/ Product	Location	Total # Emp.	Sample Job	# Emp. Sam. Job	% Black
Black-owned Firms							
1. Cannon Chem.	1979	Adhesives/paint	N. Central Detroit	115 (2 sites)	Paint prod.	118	197
2. Curve-All	1978	Metal stampings	Northwest Detroit	85	Press operator	154	100
3. Crowe Products	1990	Steel cutters	Westside Detroit	60	Prod. worker	130	150
4. Trail Industries	1973	Truck repair	Northwest Detroit	8	Prep worker	118	100
5. Sears Metals	1975	Metal fabricators	Southwest Detroit	47	Entry-prod.	110	190
6. Satellite Fasteners	1989	Fastener production	East Detroit	36	Set-up trainee	113	133
7. Morgan Stamping	1975	Metal stampings	N. Central Detroit	24	Press operator	114	187
8. Silver Inc.	1982	Plastic parts (1992)	Northwest Detroit	65	Packer	117	172
9. CalOrange	1975	Metal parts production	Adjacent CBD	275 (2 sites)	Machine operator	190	100
10. Woodward Gas	1984	Propane gas supply	N.Central Detroit	15	Fuel Plant operator	114	
11. Elizabeth Plastics	1965 Owner: 1985	Plastic parts production	Roseville (N. suburb)	145	Machine operator	100	165
12. Lionel	1950 Owner: 1987	Plastic parts production	Roseville	205	Machine operator	132	135
13. Twain Plastics	1984	Plastic parts	Troy (N. suburb)	70	Machine operator	145	188

Table 1-1 Firm Profiles (*cont.*)

White Firms by Numbered Match

Firm	Year/Owner	Industry	Location	Employees	Job title		
1. Lackawanna	Owner: 1984	Adhesives/paint	N. Central Detroit	120 (2 sites)	Paint prod.	117	10
2. Maybee	1909	Steel fabrication	Detroit CBD	47	Entry-prod.	114	80
3. TopPoint Products	1950	Wire/tubing fabrication	Westside Detroit	40	Prod. worker	123	75
4. Flamebest	1992	Truck repair	Northwest Detroit	10	Prep. worker	115	40
5. Gratiot Welding	1959	Metal fabrication	Southwest Detroit	14	Prod. worker	112	19
6. Planet Products	1911	Fastener production	East Detroit	150	Plating operator	140	50
7. Dartmouth	1945 Owner: 1993	Metal stamping	W. Central Detroit	65	Press operator	145	35
8. Sargeant Gum	1949	Adhesive labels	Northwest Detroit	42	Packer	116	50
9. Armstrong Industries	Owner: 1941	Metal parts prod.	Northeast Detroit	215	Prod. worker	175	50
10. USG	No info.	Propane gas	Trenton (S. suburb)	10	Propane distrib.	118	10
11. Mushroom	1955	Plastic and metal parts	Warren (N. suburb)	175 (2 sites)	Machine operator	135	15
12. Janis Snap	1950	Metal parts production	Roseville (N. suburb)	75	Machine operator	116	10
13. Mash Inc.	1956	Metal parts production	Roseville	76	Machine operator	140	13

product produced; in all but one or two cases they are located in the same section of the city (i.e., north, south, east, or west Detroit).[10]

Response rates among white-owned city firms I contacted was quite good; of the 14 firms first contacted, 10 participated. White-owned suburban firms located in an area that is known for racial discrimination were most likely to refuse to participate; out of 10 firms contacted in this area, only 3 participated. I had particular difficulty with suburban personnel in the plastics industry (all 3 suburban black-owned firms—Twain, Elizabeth, and Lionel—made plastic products). One match, Twain and Mash Inc., paired a plastics firm with one that produced both plastic and metal products, though both had similar, extremely light manufacturing processes. Another case-matched pair, Lionel and Janis, matched a manufacturing processes that used plastics with one that was metal-based. However, the designated entry-level jobs for both firms were very similar and required nearly the same skills.

Finally, because of the difficulty of convincing white-owned suburban firms to participate, Twain's match, Mash Inc., was located 6 miles closer the city of Detroit. The fact that Mash Inc., a white-owned firm with a nearly totally white workforce, was matched with a suburban firm with a majority-black workforce that was located much further from Detroit's black population, provided an interesting twist on minority hiring in the context of spatial mismatch theory, which will be discussed in detail in chapter 3.

In addition, I completed interviews with several informants from organizations that deal directly with employment issues as they affect urban minority youth in the southeast Michigan area.

THE SURVEY INSTRUMENT AND
THE INTERVIEW PROCESS

The survey instrument initially used was prepared in collaboration with researchers for the MCSUI project (one of whom worked on Wilson's project as well. The structure of the instrument included an initial focus on skills, locational discrimination, "journey to work" issues, and questions on gender issues. To help diffuse heightened employer sensitivity to race issues, I asked the transitional question (also used in the Wilson and MCSUI surveys) to lead into race issues: "you may know, blacks are doing far worse in the labor market now than they have in recent years; why do you think this is so?"

As can be seen in table 1-2, I completed a total of 52 interviews at 26 firms: 13 white-owned and 13 black-owned. The length of the interviews

Table 1-2 Respondent Profiles

Black-owned Firms

Firm Name	Respondent	Position	Race	Gender	Age (appr.)	Yrs./firm
1. Cannon Chem.	Dell Glenn	Majority Owner/CEO	Black	Male	58	15
	Nyab Muam	Supervisor	Black	Male	35	4
2. Curve-All	Thad Ransom	Operations manager	Black	Male	40	10
	William Indigo	Floor supervisor	Black	Male	32	10
3. Crowe Products	Patricia Manning	Personnel director	Black	Female	30	4
	Jim Schmidt	Floor supervisor	White	Male	35	4
4. Trail Industries	Sylvia Pratt	Vice president	Black	Female	58	20
	Howard Pratt	Oper. manager	Black	Male	30	10
5. Sears Metals	Debra Louis	Majority owner/CEO	Black	Female	45	15
	Bob Cantwell	Pt. owner/supervisor	White	Male	40	6
6. Satellite Fasteners	Bill Loman	Majority owner/CEO	Black	Male	65	20*
	Virgil Wolfe	Prod. manager	White	Male	60	14
7. Morgan Stamping	Caroline Simon	Full owner/CEO	Black	Female	45	8
	Tom Amodio	Floor supervisor	White	Male	50	<1
8. Silver Inc.	Ron Silver	President and CEO	Black	Male	60	23
	Denise Waring	Personnel manager	Black	Female	45	2
	Fred Renning	Supervisor	White	Male	50	14 mo.
9. CalOrange	Greg Thinge	Head of operations	White	Male	42	3.5
	Helen Haley	Personnel director	Black	Female	28	3
10. Woodward	Mick Findott	Owner	Black	Male	62	10

Firm Name	Respondent	Position	Race	Gender	Age (appr.)	Yrs./ firm
11. Elizabeth Plastic Products	Micky Taylor	Personnel director	Black	Female	45	5
	Ron Betz	Floor supervisor	White	Male	52	15
12. Lionel Plastics	Carl Johnson	Majority owner/CEO	Black	Male	62	7
	Marie Scrimo	Personnel director	White	Female	38	14
	Sol Bird	Floor supervisor	Black	Male	30	4
13. Twain Plastics	Jim Twain	Owner and CEO	Black	Male	50	11
	Tom Coles	Floor supervisor	Black	Male	26	3
White-owned Matches (by Number)						
1. Lackawanna	Ken Vetter	President	White	Male	48	3
	Dan Mulvay	Personnel director	White	Male	52	1
	Dave Devarti	Plant manager	White	Male	50	10
2. Maybee	Lester Maybee	Head of operations	White	Male	50	14
	Jerry Rivers	Floor supervisor	White	Male	50	4
3. TopPoint Products	Mike Rourke	Plant manager	White	Male	52	4
4. Flamebest	Paul Paris	Co-owner/super.	White	Male	48	1
5. Gratiot Welding	Jim Gratiot	Owner/supervisor	White	Male	35	17
6. Planet Products	Peter Flynn	CEO	White	Male	52	22
	Joe Radoccia	Personnel director	White	Male	42	18
	Kevin Peele	Floor supervisor	White	Male	32	6 mo.
7. Dartmouth	Jim Marrow	CEO	White	Male	45	5
	Mike Looney	Floor supervisor	White	Male	36	1

White-owned Matches (by Number) *(cont.)*

Firm Name	Respondent	Position	Race	Gender	Age (appr.)	Yrs./ firm
8. Sargeant Gum	Jim Morris	President and CEO	White	Male	68	45
	Dan Stack	Head of operations	White	Male	50	24
9. Armstrong Industries	William Romeo	Personnel director	White	Male	50	2
	Felix Mendell	Production mngr.	White	Male	45	25
10. USG	Warren Herland	Manager	White	Male	35	7
11. Mushroom	Bruce Johnstone	Owner/CEO	White	Male	48	12
	Gretchen Toles	Personnel director	White	Female	32	4
12. Janis Snap	Linus Metzger	CEO	White	Male	48	10
	Jim Hesse	Plant manager	White	Male	35	4
	Tim Tielman	Floor supervisor	White	Male	34	14
13. Mash Inc.	George Zarycky	CEO	White	Male	45	18

*Loman and Wolfe were with the parent firm (Planet Products) for all but the past 4 years.

ranged from one hour to over 5 hours (the average interview lasted about 90 minutes). The CEO was interviewed in 18 of the 26 firms. Unlike the Wilson project, where only representatives from upper-level management were interviewed, I sought interviews with floor supervisors who had day-to-day contact with entry-level workers at each firm, as well as the CEO or director and the head of personnel.

In 4 of the 26 firms (the white-owned Mushroom, Sergeant Gum, and Mash Inc., as well as the black-owned Cal Orange Inc.), access to a floor supervisor was denied. I averaged two respondents per firm; in the smaller firms one or two individuals often play multiple roles.

ANALYSIS

Using the Case-Match Format

Each black-owned firm was matched to a white-owned firm in terms of technology used, location, size, and product produced. This case-by-case match controls for racial ownership differences, and also firm location, skill changes, and firm size. Due to the small sample size, this analysis is mostly qualitative in nature.[11]

Interviews were taped, transcribed, and edited. Analysis consisted of pattern-matching responses on each research topic by case match and looking for consistent differences between pairs. If significant and consistent differences in responses occur between each matched black-white pair across cases, I have what Yin describes as "theoretical replication."

Theoretical replication does not provide a means to generalize findings to larger populations; however, it is considered a means to provide valid qualitative findings if certain theoretical precepts vary consistently between matches. Because the selection of participants is not random, this methodology does not provide a means to generalize findings to larger populations; however, as Yin emphasizes, it is considered a means to provide valid qualitative findings.

NOTES

[1]Direct evidence of housing discrimination is presented in Fix and Struyk (1993) and Turner (1991). As of 1980, about one-third of all blacks living in SMSA's now live in the suburbs, although the fraction is less in large metropolitan areas, especially in the Northeast (23.3 percent) and Midwest (19.3 percent). In spite of some blacks moving to the suburbs, their housing remains largely segre-

gated from that of whites. As measured by a variety of indices, segregation of black housing fell slightly in the 1970s, but it remains far higher than for Hispanic and Asian immigrants (Massey and Denton, 1989). In some cities, such as Detroit and New York City, residential segregation indices have actually grown from 1980 to 1990 (Farley, 1994). Evidence for employment discrimination will be presented in detail in chapter 7. It should also be noted that as early as 1963, over half of the employment in retail and manufacturing was suburbanized. Now, over 75 percent of manufacturing jobs are located in suburban areas (Holzer, 1991).

[2]For an excellent analysis of this complex issue see Waldinger (1993).

[3]A recent article in *Crain's Detroit Business* (Arkeny, 1997) notes that the mayor of Detroit, Dennis Archer, reported to the city council that nearly six thousand vacant buildings require demolition in the city; an additional twenty-five hundred empty buildings are sealed and could be rehabilitated, if funds were available.

[4]To this day, because of the racially biased design of training and apprenticeship programs, which lean heavily on the recommendations of white workers, blacks continue to have difficulty in breaking into the skilled trades; this issue is further addressed in chapter 6.

[5]All firm and respondent names are pseudonyms.

[6]Although, of course, I had no way of determining just how much; I also had no way of knowing who set wages, and why certain levels were selected.

[7]Although Wilson's 1997 book *When Work Disappears* downplays the role of racial discrimination in the employment problems of blacks (particularly that of young black men), this research also led to the earlier publication of Kirschenman and Neckerman's *We'd Love to Hire Them But,* a much-quoted piece that states that a job applicant's race is the key determinant in employer hiring decisions. I will address Wilson's work in more detail in chapter 6. Also see Turner Meiklejohn, 1999.

[8]The survey instrument I used was developed with Joleen Kirschenman, who was a researcher on both the Wilson and MCSUI projects; I also used it for my MCSUI interviews.

[9]This case-match format was prescribed by Yin (1989).

[10]This effort was hampered by several factors. First, there are very few white-owned auto parts suppliers located in the city of Detroit. For one black-owned firm—Woodward Gas—there was not a single white-owned comparable firm in the city. A suburban firm (USG, in the suburb of Trenton) was chosen instead. In another case—Silver Plastics—there were no firms making the same product within city boundaries. A firm that made adhesive labels was chosen to be its match.

[11]This study proceeds in a case study format described by Robert Yin (1989).

CHAPTER 2

Racial Segregation in the Detroit Metropolitan Area
A Long-Lived and Persistent Phenomenon

Residential suburbanization began late in the nineteenth century in the Detroit area and continued through the first decades of the twentieth century. It was fueled by changes in building technology, cheap land, and higher wages that allowed waves of first- and second-generation immigrants to own a home of their own. However, even with a crushing housing shortage in Detroit brought on by the waves of African American migration to the city during World War I, racial discrimination kept African Americans from entering the housing market on the same terms as other groups before them. And it was not only poor blacks who were unable to make inroads into home ownership; the urban historian Kenneth Jackson writes that "the most striking feature of black life was not slum conditions, but the barriers that middle-class blacks encountered in trying to escape the ghetto" (Jackson, 1985).

By the 1920s blacks were increasingly relegated to "Black Bottom," Detroit's already overcrowded ghetto, located immediately northeast of the central business district. During this time suburban communities began to incorporate on their own, in part because sharper ethnic and class divisions were occurring in the city. These divisions sometimes erupted into violence, such as in the case of Ossian Sweet, a black physician. In the early 1920s a mob of several hundred whites sought forcibly to eject Sweet and his family from a house he had bought just outside the borders of the Bottom. When Sweet and his brother took up arms and killed a man while defending the household, he was charged of murder. Sweet was successfully defended by Clarence Darrow.

Suburbanization was hastened in the early decades of this century by automobile availability and affordability; which was especially true in the area known as Motor City. The growth of car ownership was accompanied by massive road building. The Federal Highway Act of 1910 offered funds to states with organized highway departments, and by 1925 the value of highway construction exceeded one billion dollars for the first time. By the 1920s, GM bought and demolished most of the trolley system in Detroit in order to force the use of buses that they manufactured. With the advent of the automobile, residential suburbanization blossomed in metropolitan Detroit in the 1920s.

Concurrent with residential suburbanization was an equal growth of industrial suburbanization. As early as 1934 one household head in eight journeyed to work from one suburb to another (Jackson, 1985). Factories had begun to move out of city areas with the advent of steam power in 1859, but from 1915-1930, the number of trucks grew from 158,000 to 3.5 million, which allowed factories independence from locations along rail lines. New methods of materials handling emphasized one-story construction, and industry decentralization altered spatial patterns of metropolitan areas.

The long process of the de-industrialization of northern and midwestern industrial cities actually began as early as 1920-1930, when the proportion of central-city factory employment declined in every major city with population over one hundred thousand (Jackson, 1985). Warehousing and distribution concerns followed factories to urban edges where almost all new factory construction took place after 1925. These are facts to consider when assessing the work of authors who see the industrial decline of American cities a relatively recent phenomenon (Jackson, 1985; Wilson, 1987; Kasarda, 1988).

Segregation Becomes Federal Policy: the 1930s-1940s

It was not just the benign preference of white city residents for the green lawns and quiet streets of the suburbs that was responsible for the stark division between largely minority urban centers and white suburbs that we see today in Detroit and similar cities: it was federal housing policy that intensified and institutionalized black-white segregation.

In 1933 the Home Owners Loan Corporation (HOLC) was formed in urban areas to protect against foreclosure and relieve excessive interest and principal incurred in these predepression years. It was then that the federal government began the systematic practice of redlining—race and ethnicity became defining criteria for participation in this program.

This process was the first pervasive federal institutionalization of discrimination.

In 1934, the National Housing Act created the Federal Housing Administration (FHA) which was later supplemented by the Servicemen's Readjustment Act of 1944 (the GI bill). These programs were the first to enforce HOLC discriminatory policy and procedures. Factors that were considered most important on this rating scale included the neighborhood's "relative economic stability and protection from adverse influences." Older neighborhoods, heterogeneous environments, and "inharmonious racial or nationality groups" were excluded from consideration; this legislation mandated rigid black-white separation. It also endorsed "suitable restrictive covenants" (Jackson, 1985, p. 197).

The acts fostered the construction of white suburban neighborhoods while simultaneously hastening inner-city decay, for they financed the construction of new homes and only provided small loans for home repair. The FHA then charted the present and likely future location of black families—one black family on any block would preempt the entire block from program participation.

At this time in the city of Detroit, racial tension over housing broke into large-scale physical fights in 1942, when blacks attempted to move into the Sojourner Truth homes in central Detroit. From 1942-1943 over 345,000 migrants—black and white—arrived from the South to work in defense plants. By 1943, a race riot erupted near the Belle Isle bridge. Nine whites and 25 blacks were killed as federal troops were called in.

In 1948, one of the country's first suburban enclosed malls, Northland Shopping Center, opened in suburban Detroit. In 1949, a new federal law proposed that new public housing units were not to be built on less costly land outside central cities (as in Europe). Public housing was legally confined to existing slums and the image of suburbia remained.

The Interstate Highway Act of 1956 allowed the construction of a $26 billion, 42,500-mile highway system that further facilitated white out-migration to the suburbs. In the case of the city of Detroit, the physical implementation of its intricate highway system helped further to disrupt and destroy black neighborhoods.

Retail out-migration rapidly followed residential and industrial out-migration. Jackson writes that the "most famous retailing victim of the drive-in culture thus far has been the J. L. Hudson company in Detroit. It was a simple fact that all roads in the Motor City led to Hudson's. The 25 story, full block emporium ranked with Macy's in NY and Marshall Field's in Chicago as one of the country's three largest stores." After

1950, the store was "choked by its branches in outlying shopping centers" (Jackson, 1985, pp. 260-261). The opening of Northland, which included the chain's biggest suburban outlet, in 1948, drove downtown Detroit's Hudson's sales from $153 million in 1953 to $45 million in 1981 (in constant dollars). In spite of the work of the liberal Cavanaugh administration, a race riot erupted in Detroit in 1967. Federal troops were called in. Thirty-three blacks and 10 whites were killed. This event precipitated a flood of white residential and commercial outmigration from the city of Detroit.

Detroit in the Context of National Trends

Housing segregation for blacks remained high in the 1970s even for blacks with higher incomes and for those living in the suburbs. Logan and Schneider (1982) show that, in Northern Standard Metropolitan Statistical Areas (SMSAs), black migrants in the 1970s were most likely to locate in communities that were close to the central city and already had a high incidence of black residents. Frey (1984) notes that the pattern of selective black migration to the suburbs in the 1970s was similar to that of whites in the 1950s and '60s—that is, migration in both cases was concentrated among younger and better-educated residents of inner cities.

In 1970, the gap between educational attainments of suburban and central-city residents was substantially higher for whites than for blacks. However, by 1980, the greatest gains in educational attainment among blacks had occurred among those residing in the suburbs; the suburban-city gap in education among blacks was now higher than that among whites.

Although many blacks have moved to suburbs, their housing remains largely segregated from that of whites. Regarding this segregation of black housing, a variety of indices show that there was virtually no change within the largest metropolitan areas of the northeast and Midwest (Massey and Denton, 1989).

By 1980, 60 percent of metropolitan populations lived outside of the central city. By 1983, two-thirds of all manufacturing took place in "industrial parks" and new physical plants in the suburbs. Employers were lured out by promises of open land, access to interstate highways, and federal tax incentives.

Although overall employment in manufacturing has generally declined relative to the financial, trade, and service sectors, the greatest decline in manufacturing occurred in central-city areas. Kasarda (1988), reports that in the six largest SMSAs of the Northeast and Midwest, manufacturing employment fell by about 352,000 in the central cities and rose by about 200,000 in the suburbs. In addition, nonmanufacturing employment fell by 202,000 in the central cities and rose by 333,000 in the suburbs.

As of 1980, about one-third of all blacks living in SMSAs now live in the suburbs, although the fraction is less in large metropolitan areas, especially in the Northeast (23.3 percent) and Midwest (19.3 percent; Massey and Denton, 1988.) Jackson (1985) writes that in the 1980s:

> ... the most conspicuous city-suburban contrast in the United States runs along Detroit's Alter Road. Residents call the street the "Berlin Wall" or "the barrier" or "the Mason-Dixon Line." It divides the suburban Grosse Pointe communities from the east side of Detroit, which is poor and mostly black. The Detroit side is studded with abandoned cars, graffiti-covered schools, and burned-out buildings. Two blocks away, within view, are neatly clipped hedges and immaculate houses. ... On the one side, says John Kelly, a Democratic state senator whose district awkwardly straddles both neighborhoods, is "west Beirut" on the other side, "Disneyland."

In the 1980s, over 80 percent of the overall black population was urban. The cycle of decline had already begun in the inner suburbs. Some, like Oak Park, Michigan, which sprang up in the 1950s along Detroit's northern boundary, are prospering because of unusual religious and racial diversity. Others are encountering fiscal, educational, racial, and housing crises as severe as those that troubled major cities in the 1960s and 70s.

It has also been determined that in the 1980s significantly higher employment growth rates were found in suburban areas relative to central cities, and that the wages for less-skilled jobs appear to be higher in the suburbs, which supports the notion that labor demand is higher and the market is tighter in suburban areas (Vroman and Peterson, 1993).

By 1990, blacks made up 76 percent of the Detroit's population of 1,028,000. Ninety-two percent of Detroit's three-county metropolitan area's white population live in the suburban ring, while only 8 percent live in the city of Detroit (only 222,000 whites remained in the city). Seventeen percent of area's blacks live in the suburbs and 83 percent live in the city. Twenty-four percent of the Detroit metropolitan area is black; only 5 percent of the suburban ring's population is black.

Detroit has most severe city-suburban segregation of all the major metropolises of one million or more population in the United States. The metropolitan area's dissimilarity index is 88, meaning that 88 percent of the population would have to move to create an equal dispersion of blacks and whites. The magnitude of this index has remained virtually unchanged in the past 20 years. The indices of segregation are uniform across both educational attainment and family income categories; in fact, the dissimilarity index score rises slightly with educational attainment and family income—underscoring how only mostly poor and poorly educated whites remain in the city of Detroit. The Detroit metropolitan area is the only area with a population over five hundred thousand where segregation increased in the 1980s (Farley, Steeh and Krysan, 1994).

Since the city of Detroit is almost completely black, and its suburbs are nearly completely white, the following data are particularly telling when assessing the impact of segregation. The census reported that a typical white household in the Detroit SMSA had an income of $46,100, while a typical black's income was $26,900. This racial discrepancy is getting larger: in 1980 black households in Detroit had incomes that were 65 percent those of whites; in 1990, the figure was only 58 percent. Overall in Detroit, black poverty increased from 26 to 38 percent of all households; among whites it climbed from 6 to 8 percent. Eleven percent of white children were in poverty, and 44 percent of black children were impoverished (United States Census, 1990).

CHAPTER 3

Employer Location Decisions
Detroit's Image and Actuality

It may be helpful for the understanding of study findings—which point to the fact that the boundaries of the city appear to define a labor market that is separate from those of the surrounding suburbs—to present how the city of Detroit is perceived by employers. The words of employers indicate—both directly and obliquely—that the fact that the city is majority black affects their perceptions about the city and the people that live there. In other words, the image of the city affects outsiders' views about the people who live there and, according to some employers, the image of the city also affects self-image. A negative place image affects employment-location decisions as well as hiring decisions. Here I examine what a Detroit location means for the employers who have left the city and those who have chosen to remain there. I asked Detroit employers why they decided to locate where they are, what they think about their current location, and how they think customers and outsiders view the city of Detroit.

WHITE-OWNED DETROIT FIRMS: RATIONALE FOR THEIR CURRENT LOCATION

Because so few of the Detroit metropolitan area's employers remain within city boundaries, it is important to understand why some firms chose to locate or remain there. Among surveyed white-owned firms, the reasons for remaining in the city are clear: 8 out of 9 surveyed firms stated that it is too costly and complicated to move.[1] In addition, two firms were about to close, while two others had shut down within 18 months of being interviewed. With the exception of two respondents, none indicated that if they had their way, they would remain in the city of Detroit.

One white city-based respondent who appeared to indicate a clear preference for his city location on the northern city border, the president of Sargeant Gum,[2] stated that he chose to locate in the city as an expression of both his economic and religious beliefs. He felt that the creation of a workable business within the boundaries of a "ghetto" would not only prove his economic prowess, but was also the best way of expressing his religious convictions, which placed a high value on economic and racial justice:

> Well, this was important to me, there's not really much more to say than the fact that I felt the importance of having industry as a base where people could earn monies and then spend the monies in their own communities as opposed to having the money earned and flown out of the community. . . .

However, the firm's vice president, when asked about the positives and negatives of the current location, replied: "Positives, number one is Ford Motor Company. Ford Motor Company likes to have suppliers with the Detroit address" (they are dealing with six divisions of Ford Motor Company). When asked whether he ever thought of moving, he answered, "oh, yeah." When I asked where, he said, "someplace else." He also noted that the company was prepared to move recently (something the president never mentioned), but the suburban site they had chosen was found to be contaminated with toxic wastes.

DIRTY INDUSTRIES (TOXIC
MATERIALS AND PROCESSES)

Detroit white employers are reluctant residents. One common explanation for a city location was that their industry was "dirty," and that moving or closing required an expensive cleanup of their toxic sites. Four white city firms fall into this category: Planet Products, Lackawanna Chemical, Maybee Industries, and Armstrong Industries. The cost of cleanup might be relevant (even though it was not mentioned) for several white-owned firms that said they were located in Detroit because of tradition and history, as they also dealt with hazardous processes and materials.

Among the 19 city firms (with both white and black owners), 17 appeared to deal with toxic manufacturing processes (one exception recently retooled from dirty to more automated and cleaner processes, but did not move). These processes include glue and paint production (2 firms), metal finishing, repair and processing using less automated production processing (13 firms), and inflammable gas (one firm). Only 3 firms appeared to use the cleaner, more automated production processes found in 6 of 7 suburban firms surveyed.

It is not the case that dirty industries were clustered within city boundaries because the city of Detroit, in order to retain or attract firms, had less stringent environmental requirements than other localities. The president of Lackawanna Chemical reported that the Department of Natural Resources (DNR) is actually more difficult to accommodate in the city than in the surrounding suburbs:

> Wayne county is one of the toughest. Now, we deal in chlorinated solvents, which is that nasty stuff, trichlorifline and so on and so forth. Wayne is much tougher on how you have a lab, than Oakland, Macomb, Monroe. . . . So that makes it somewhat difficult with our technology in the city.

He felt there were dirty industries within city boundaries because "they got there first and it's difficult to move, it's expensive to move. If you're already on a site, if you own the property, the day that you decide to move off, and somebody else buys the property, you have to analyze the soil." In fact, legislation does not require owners to complete soil analyses or rid their properties of contaminants *unless* they attempt to sell or move. He considers this:

> You see, the EPA really is, talk about foolish, they ought to say, analyze your soil, find out what the problems are, define the problem, and then work out a program to fix it. Right now, if you don't know that you have a problem, you are almost a fool to analyze it because as soon as you know you have a problem you have to immediately fix it. Now, let's say you're sitting on a small little facility that's been on the same piece of property for 70 years, which we got some of those, as a matter of fact; we've been on it for 70 years, and we suspect there might be some junk down there, but we don't know. As long as you don't know, you don't have to do anything about it. . . .

This is the reason that an additional 3 of the 9 white-owned city firms gave me in explanation of their Detroit address. For example, the manufacturing manager at Armstrong Industries told me that:

> Right now, you're looking at a white elephant. This building. Years ago, we thought, my God, if the company sold it to Chrysler, the first thing they would do is tear it down and make it a parking lot. . . . They don't want us, nobody would want this right here . . . and what have you got when you're done, if you do purchase this building? Underneath here, years ago we had gasoline tanks, we had our own tanks, this and that in there, and we've filled those with sand. I don't know environmentally-wise what you're sitting on here is a keg of dynamite.

When a large corporation recently attempted to buy the operation, the manager said that:

> [O]ur philosophy on that was, no, we ain't taking no ground samples, we don't want to know what you've got, so if you want the place, it's yours. But we don't want it. Oh yeah, they were going to buy the business, but I don't know what they were going to do with this site . . . it's a white elephant. And what are you going to do with it? You can't get a penny for this building.

He stresses, though, that the firm remains in operation in the city rather than closing, because:

> [W]ell they're not going to do that [shut down] when they're making money, for crying out loud, that would be silly . . . it's well known in the automotive industry, very good reputation in the automotive industry . . . and that's the number-one line when you talk about why does the family stay and that, because it's making money. If it didn't, believe me, like anything else, you wouldn't want it, you wouldn't keep it.

HISTORY AND TRADITION

Representatives from the four remaining white-owned firms gave simple or elaborate answers as to why they were in Detroit that revolved around the theme of "because we've always been here." For example, the CEO of Dartmouth Stamping noted that his parent corporation recently bought the firm because they "wanted a Detroit location" (the previous owners had been there for 50 years: after the completion of this interview the firm changed ownership twice and finally shut down in 1995).

WHITE-OWNED FIRMS: CONCERNS
ABOUT IMAGE AND SAFETY

Representatives from 5 of the 9 white-owned city firms described fears about the area on the part of customers and potential employees. For example, the personnel director of Armstrong Industries stated that the "major problem" of location in an eastern industrial part of Detroit that was actually set quite apart from residential communities

> is customers' fear of coming into the city. Now that is a big problem, I can tell you that we have several customers who come here at night, because their parts need to be dropped off so that they're ready for the next morning, that is a very, very big problem right now . . . [a]nd it hasn't been because there's been a frequency of crime, I think that it's just the perception.

The company's CEO also noted that: "I think in the suburbs you get . . . more people that will apply. A lot of people come down to Detroit and look one time and that's the end of the process. They're not interested in being here, or if they're young, their parents are not interested in having them here." However, unlike his personnel director, the CEO feels that the customers "do not care at all" about their city location, since they are not retail and arrive in semitrucks, but workers are quite uncomfortable:

> . . . in terms of workers, when we get our general office in Detroit, they will get calls during certain upheavals from husbands saying I don't want my wife down there today, why don't you guys move your office, that kind of stuff. In recruiting employees, it makes it difficult. . . . We have to sometimes convince Joe that it will be safe here, that kind of thing.

Lackawanna Chemical is located about a mile from Armstrong Industries. The plant manager described the negatives of his location as follows:

Customers really, well, we have corporate offices . . . all over the country. Detroit location, I mean you drive around the block and you look at the neighborhoods, this is nowhere where you want one of your Ford, GM, Chrysler automotive purchasing people to come by. Even with a little more dressing up on the plant, which we've done in the past, you're still next to the neighborhood. Given there's a broken toilet across the street over there, you know, there's tires lying, very negative. Crime, break-ins, very negative.

However, he emphasized that the real negative was (suburban) customer perceptions about the area, rather than the reality of the area. When I asked if his neighborhood was unsafe, he replied:

Not really, okay? It's got a problem with theft. Murders, rape, stuff like that, for being in the city of Detroit, I feel comfortable . . . you know, I mean I keep my eyes open, but I'm not to the point where I feel we have to keep the gates shut and everything locked and whatnot. . . . So, from a crime standpoint, but there's a perception that people get, in the neighborhood where the crime isn't even actually that bad, people presume it is, for being in this location. Strong negative.

He notes that there are good neighborhoods in Detroit "and I'm not talking about Indian Village" (a well-known, middle-class neighborhood). This plant manager thinks, however, that the neighborhood has recently declined, and that this deterioration has been "recent, and I would say it's probably been as recent as late '80s." When I asked why he though this was so, he blamed outside perceptions for instilling a sense of hopelessness in area residents:

I don't know if it's media issues, if it's just an awareness in the public, and that's a personal thing that irritates me. You know, you get through it, somebody gets shot from a car, all of a sudden Detroit is don't drive on the freeways. . . . The image of Detroit is so rotten. And I think people inside it have felt it's so rotten there's no way to, there's no hope. It's that everything that happens here, something bad goes on. And then when it does, it's keyed on, it's keyed on, it's keyed on. . . . What runs through everybody's mind? I'm never going to go to Detroit. I think there's just a lot more issues, especially more recently, carjackings, I don't know.

The comments of the manager of Lackawanna's are especially interesting when juxtaposed against those of his parent corporation's CEO. This respondent, who took this job 2 years ago, is ensconced in an office in suburban Southfield. His fears about going to the city of Detroit are typical of the suburbanites described by his city plant manager:

> To be quite frank with you, I drove today to one of our Detroit facilities, and I had to drive the Suburban. I would not drive a more precious vehicle into the city. When I go down to dinner, at Joe Muir's or something like that, which I like, I purposely pick a vehicle that's not very attractive. I don't want to be carjacked or anything. I would assume that our employees feel the same way, particularly the ones that are hard-working, etc.

The CEO of Maybee Industries described a general theme about potential workers: they drive to the plant for an interview, take one look, and drive away without going inside:

> Detroit is not an attractive place in their mind. It has a fairly well-established reputation. Our headquarters here is not any great neighborhood, we kind of consider ourselves a little oasis. We have in fact had people show up for interviews and continue to drive on.

Maybee's drop forge supervisor has far more complaints about their location than his boss, including terrible city services, unresponsive police, disgruntled workers, and crime. But when I asked him whether his location was worse or better than he anticipated, he said emphatically: "It's not as bad. It's not as bad. I think a lot of it's media hype, I think they paint us to be very, very bad."

One of the most interesting respondents from a white-owned plant was a supervisor who had just changed jobs from a firm in a poor white suburb to his current position in the city firm Planet Products. When I asked him to compare the positives and negatives of the two locations he stressed that it was not just that he thought Detroit was unsafe (a fact he says he is getting used to), but that the quality of life of his city workers was disturbing and depressing. He relates that he began to understand what these workers were going through by

> probably just talking to the people, cause it's really so hard to deal with this, it's everyday life for them . . . you just drive down in the morning,

at 7 o'clock in the morning and see the little kids walking to school, they're walking by burned-out houses. . . . Myself, I have a good home life, I leave here, I go down to Southgate and I got a nice home, I got two boys. I think a lot of it's something to deal with where do you go after work, what's your life outside of this place, cause if you have no plans or goals or something outside, I mean if your home life's trash, why care about anything?

It should be noted that while white employers with city locations were often quite voluble about what they thought to be the disadvantages of a Detroit location, they also stressed that they thought the reality of Detroit is not as bad as the perceptions of the city by customers and potential suburban workers, and were far less likely than white suburban respondents to denigrate the city. In fact, *all* the interviewed individuals in the 9 white-owned city-based firms in this sample made a point of saying that the media and suburbanites portrayed the city as a far worse place than it actually is.

BLACK-OWNED FIRMS

Among the black-owned firms, the reasons for a Detroit location are more varied: some are there because of the firm owner's commitment to the city, and others because it is less expensive to operate and to acquire property in the city, even without incentives.

A Commitment to the City of Detroit and its People

The CEOs of three minority-owned businesses—Silver, CalOrange, and Cannon Chemical, Inc.—all stated that their location in the city was to benefit the community economically and provide jobs to African-American residents. The CEO of Cannon Chemical moved his operations to the city 10 years ago. He notes: "We had one of our companies out in the suburbs and when space became available in the city, we moved that company into the city." When asked whether this was due primarily to a cost equation or a commitment factor, he responded:

It was primarily a commitment factor. We knew what the costs were and we think that they balance out reasonably well. . . . Well, in terms of what we've done, in terms of our own personal dollars, okay, I have a choice between putting up investment across the street or looking for space outside of the city, and our commitment is to the city so we do it here.

The CEO of Silver expanded this notion of commitment; he considered his operation a sort of training program. Because he has relatively few positions for promotions for his relatively high proportion of low-skilled workers, his intent was to provide training so that young black residents would qualify for jobs elsewhere. He even makes the connections for them. He stated that because his workers knew that they had future prospects, not necessarily in his own plant but in other plants, they worked especially hard. In a characteristic self-deprecating manner, he noted that this decision also served "selfish reasons as well."

Opportunities for Black Entrepreneurship: Decreased Land and Operating Costs

The CEO of Woodward Gas cited the fact that Detroit offers far more opportunities to black businessmen than other locations:

> I feel great about Detroit, I don't think we would have been as successful, especially being a minority company, anywhere else . . . [when] I was a minority person in greater Chicago land, I found there weren't that many [opportunities], whereas in Detroit, Michigan you find a large number of Hispanic, black, Asian business people. That's the only large city I've had experience with outside of Detroit, so those are the two I have to compare.

The CEO of Morgan Stamping also notes that the decision to move to Detroit from the smaller city of Ypsilanti was pragmatic. In Detroit they could afford to purchase a structure, rather than lease one, and they liked being "closer to our customers and suppliers." The director of personnel of Crowe Products, a newly established minority-owned firm, echoed this sentiment.

Respondents from Sears Fabricating stated that cost concerns were a key factor for a move back to the city. The co-owner and supervisor stated:

> We could never survive outside of the city, because with this business, the competition we have to deal with . . . anybody that's gone outside of the city to try and operate, it seems like they always come back because they can't afford to. The property taxes are much higher, and because of the competition in this business, it's hard to pay a big high wage, and it seems like the people outside the city demand a higher wage.[3]

The CEO at Curve-All emphasized:

A lot of people stay (in Detroit) for economical reasons. The building's probably paid for, and you know the property in Detroit is pretty cheap compared to . . . the suburbs. You take this plant right here and move it down to Livonia (a growing suburban location) somewhere, the taxes would be twice as much, the building would be twice as much.

What Respondents in Black-Owned Firms Think about Detroit

Black respondents also acknowledged the perception and actuality of the city as unsafe. For example, the CEO of Cannon Chemical (which chooses a city location) stated:

Oh, I think people have an image of Detroit that is crime-laden, and I think that there's some accuracy to that, not that that's not valid for other urban centers. . . . But I think it makes it difficult if you're really trying to attract top talent who don't know much about the city, and they are saying, you know, I don't know whether I want to bring my wife and kids into that kind of environment, you know, maybe I'll just work someplace else. I've had IRS agents say that they considered us to be a, I guess what they call a battle zone or whatever the heck. They've red-zoned the Detroit area, and if you are an IRS agent during an audit you have the right to request special kinds of assistance when you're doing an audit in the city and depending on where the business is located, if they don't give this particular agent the kind of support he's talking about, an armed guard or whatever, he doesn't have to do it.

However, the CEO of Cannon Chemical also notes that lower operating costs in the city override his concern about the perceptions of outsiders: "The good part about . . . our location here, is that it's inexpensive because property values are certainly quite depressed. You can get very inexpensive property here."

In addition, the head of personnel at Crowe Industries notes that representatives from the temp agency she uses state that potential workers turn down jobs in Detroit:

[T]hat's what they're telling us, that people that'll come into their [suburban] offices because they are not located in Detroit, that when they ask individuals, tell them about where we're located, that some of them aren't willing to come in for the interview.

They are the one firm in this sample that have chosen a city location because of state- and city-sponsored tax incentives.

However, not all interviewed black employers favored a city location, in spite of the lower operating costs associated with it. The CEO of Twain Industries recently moved from a suburb on Detroit's border to the northwestern suburb of Troy. He spoke about Detroit, his experiences in his previous, as well as his current, location, and stated that he has given the issue of a suburban versus a Detroit location a lot of thought. He emphasizes that he perceived a stark contrast between Detroit and its surrounding suburbs. He presents an interesting analogy for his refusal, as a black business owner, to be relegated to a location in Detroit—the "kitchen" of the fine restaurant of the greater metropolitan area:

> I want to say that I get involved in a lot of different places, and I travel to many other urban areas. I don't find the disparity between the city and the suburbs and black and whites as great as I find it in the Michigan area. Think of the best restaurants in Michigan and you won't see a black waiter . . . that doesn't happen accidentally. That happens because there's a perception that's established and carried forward that blacks don't belong out of the kitchen. And that's the same attitude that's at work in American industry now, that blacks don't belong out of Detroit or Pontiac, and we don't belong in management positions. We can own it because the car companies have these minority programs, but we're not capable of running them.

This owner echoes the observations of black and white city employers when he remarks that customers appear to prefer a suburban location. He says that the biggest advantage of his (suburban) Troy location "is that my customers are more comfortable," and further notes that customer preferences, along with racial considerations, would make a city location unfeasible:

> I can't reach the business objectives that we want without having a black-owned and operated business and also have it tucked into the middle of Detroit, because my customers are not black.

Existing Land and Lower Operating Costs Do Not Offset Negative Perceptions about the City and/or a Desire to Leave Detroit

Although both black and white employers say that crime in the city is not

near the high level that it is perceived to be by the media or suburban residents, the image of the city is said to be bad. Among the sample of
white-owned city firms, even the single respondent that professed a commitment to Detroit (Sergeant Gum) has looked elsewhere and was ready
to move if his selected suburban site had not been found to be contaminated. Representatives of two firms (Lackawanna Chemical and Top-
Point Products) made it clear that they were soon shutting down, and
respondents from Maybee Industries indicated they will shut down when
their elderly founder dies. Dartmouth closed 18 months after their interview was held. Planet Products and Gratiot can't afford the costs of moving, and Armstrong Industries tried to sell its toxic site and failed. Out of
9 white-owned firms, only one owner seemed satisfied, because "it
makes no difference" to him.

The negative image of the city as perceived by customers and employees is the reason why white employers wish to move elsewhere;
white employers also stress that what they consider to be its actual negative characteristics—its crime, vacancy, and the hard lives of its residents—also gets them down. However, these employers all stated that
the city is not as bad as it is portrayed in the media or as it exists in the
minds of suburbanites.

It is clear from their statements presented here that black employers
share the perceptions of white employers in terms of the image of the
city. The foreman in the newly arrived minority-owned Crowe Products
commented about Detroit as follows: "I know Detroit's really dried up, it
really has. It's terrible to say but it's true."

In addition, black employers were very articulate about what it feels
like to work in the city. The CEO of Morgan Stamping felt that the environment in Detroit negatively influenced her and her workers:

> I'm not as eager to get up in the morning and get on into work like I
> was where I was at before. And that's because of the environment. It's
> not the best area. It's very depressing, let's say that, you know. It's not
> a way to start your day. It's not like driving down 94 to 23 Mile Road
> and Gratiot, and seeing deer out on the side of the expressway, and
> stuff like that. It's a completely different atmosphere, and I think it
> does have a lot of impact on the job. You may think that you're not
> going to let it interfere with it, but up here it does subconsciously. I
> think so.

However, black employers are also very clear about why they

wished to remain in Detroit: many were committed to the notion of its economic development and wished to benefit its minority residents.

The image of Detroit as a place, as described by these employers, points to the fact that continued racism, disinvestment, and a failure of private sector and government responsibility to improve these and other human capital and quality-of-life issues in Detroit continues to affect the image of this city and the fate of its residents. This perceived separateness of the city and its negative image may point to strategies that break down barriers and open up the suburbs, in terms of housing and jobs, as pragmatic goals to improve the economic status of minority residents.[4]

NOTES

[1]Only one respondent in this sample (Sargeant Gum) was involved in the original location decision of the firm.

[2]All respondent and firm names are pseudonyms.

[3]Only one black employer noted that lower wages accepted by city workers were a locational factor. But it should be noted that I found through my research (see Turner 1997) that among my sampleworkers in black-owned firms earned substantially less than workers in case-matched white-owned firms for jobs requiring similar skills; which, along with other cost considerations, may be a strong, if unacknowledged factor in choosing or remaining in a city location.

[4]For a more detailed discussion of the image of Detroit and respondent's location decisions in the context of recent state and federal incentive zone legislation, see Turner Meiklejohn, 1998.

CHAPTER 4

Examining Wage Differences Between Black- and White-owned Firms

The years between World War II and the mid-1960s were particularly advantageous to the labor market outcomes of African Americans: both earnings and employment rose in absolute terms, and gaps between whites and blacks in these areas narrowed considerably (Jaynes and Williams, 1989). These gains are in a large part attributable to the coalescing and influence of social-change organizations (including unions and civil rights organizations) that culminated in the enactment of the 1964 Civil Rights Act. However, it was most likely the overriding condition of a tight labor market that ensured the success of these policies.[1] The passage of the Civil Rights Act occurred at the height of the strongest economic expansion in U.S. history—from 1961-1969 economic growth occurred at the rate of 4.3 percent per year. Resulting affirmative action policies raised both the employment participation rates and earnings of black men (Leonard, 1987; Bound and Freeman, 1992). It is also important to note that as the number of jobs grew, wages rose in this period of time for all people at all wage levels. (Blank, 1998).

Many people attribute the beginning of the growth in wage and employment gaps between blacks and whites to dramatically growing earnings inequality among all workers, a process that began in the early 1970s. At this time, the combined effects of the energy crisis, inflation, and competition from newly emerging nations severely undercut the profits of American manufacturers and changed the sectoral structure of jobs.

A SHIFT FROM MANUFACTURING TO SERVICE JOBS

Between 1979 and 1987 total durable goods production declined by one
million workers (Levy, Murname, and Chen, 1993). In addition, Groshen
and Williams (1992) show that in 1990-1991, the blue-collar unemployment rate stood at 9 percent, while the white collar unemployment rate
was 4.2 percent.

In 1947, only half the population worked in the service sector, but by
the 1980s over 70 percent did (Kutscher and Personick, 1986). Newman
and Stack (1992) emphasize that most of these jobs have grown in the
low-wage part of this increasingly bifurcated (in terms of skill demands
and income) sector. For instance, after suffering a decline from 1973-
1979, the number of jobs in personal services rose from 904,444 to
1,147,000 in 1987. From 1959 to 1985, eating and drinking places alone
added 4 million jobs. Newman and Stack also cite the Bureau of Labor
Statistics predictions that virtually all net increase in jobs between mid-
1980s to the year 2000 will be the "serving producer" sector, which is the
rationale for their study that focuses on youth working at McDonald's.

TECHNOLOGICAL CHANGES

During the last two decades, technological changes have occurred at a
rapid rate in all sectors, allowing the phasing out and consolidation of
many lower-skilled service and manufacturing jobs. Meanwhile, in
many cities, legal and illegal immigrants, women, native blacks and
Hispanics are far more strongly represented in the American workforce,
increasing competition for the lower-skilled jobs that remained in these
locations in spite of a concurrent trend of industrial outsourcing. As a
result, unemployment rates and earning inequalities increased in the
1980s for *all* groups (by gender, race, and educational groupings), and
in all sectors.

INCREASING RETURNS TO SKILL

That there are clearly increasing returns to skill is supported by earnings
data disaggregated by educational level and also by data demonstrating
that employers hired workers with more education in spite of their increased cost, and hired far fewer less-educated workers even though the
wages they would have to pay them declined (Danziger and Gottschalk,
1995; Fortin and Lemieux, 1997).

There has recently been an especially stark growth in wage differentials between lesser- and more-educated workers. Wages for high school dropouts peaked in 1970 and have fallen rapidly since. High school dropouts earned 22 percent less in 1993 than they did in 1979, while high school graduates earned 12 percent less during this time period (Blank, 1998). Yet, since 1979, wages for college graduates have risen substantially: 10 percent over a 14-year period from 1979 to 1993. Postgraduates experienced a 22 percent wage increase (Blank, 1998).

The deterioration of wages for all but the most skilled workers affects men and women differently. A decline in gender discrimination has allowed the wages of all women to rise sharply; however, since 1979 wages for the least skilled women have declined by 6 percent since 1979. Still, on average, the wages for less-skilled women (averaging $287/week in 1993) are 28 percent less than those of less-skilled men (Blank, 1998).

At the time that wages were increasing for all workers in the 1960s and early 1970s, the wage gap between white and black workers was narrowing. By 1975, the gap in median wages fell from 20 percent to 5 percent. Wage growth was faster for black women than for black men, both relative to white women and white men. This progress stopped in the mid-1970s and reversed itself in the 1980s and early 1990s. By 1997, the gap in median wages between whites and blacks had grown to 17 percent (ERP, 1998).

Although there is agreement in the literature about the timing and extent of growing wage inequality among all workers, there is little agreement about its causes. Income inequality grew between groups with different observable traits, such as between more highly and less-educated workers, but also within these groups, which confounds the ability of economists to offer explanations for this phenomenon (Gottschalk, 1997). Danziger and Gottschalk (1995) emphasize that there is no single cause for increased earnings inequality. One hypothesis is that technological change has resulted in increased returns to skill. However, they note two problems with this notion. First, technical change has not been observed or measured—just inferred. Second, earnings inequality grew most in the 1980s, yet there is little direct evidence that that this was a period of rapid technological change.

In addition, there are other proposed factors causing increased earnings inequality such as the shrinking proportion of the workforce in unions and the erosion of the value of the minimum wage (Fortin and Lemieux, 1997), as well as growing workforce instability. Fewer weeks worked may not starkly effect wage inequality, but can contribute more to overall income inequality (Danziger and Gottschalk, 1995).

WAGES AND WORK EFFORT: EMPLOYMENT TRENDS AND DIFFERENTIALS

Economists have shown that wages and work behavior are closely correlated (see Juhn, 1992). In the context of growing wage and earnings inequality there are now stark differences in employment behavior between less- and more-skilled workers, and the historical trend of employment differentials between blacks and whites continues. These educational and racial differences in earnings, employment, and labor-force participation are all the more striking when viewed in the context of current economic conditions. In terms of overall employment, this is now one of the most expansive times in U.S. history. The civilian unemployment rate during the first quarter of 1999 was 4.4 percent, which is the lowest recorded rate since the 1960s. The proportion of the adult population that is now employed is the highest in history (Freeman and Rodgers, 1998).

During times of economic expansion and contraction, black workers have experienced an unemployment rate that is twice that of whites, even within comparable categories of educational attainment. For example, in 1997 the unemployment rate for black men was the lowest annual average since 1974, but at 8.4 percent it was more than double the 3.6 percent rate for white men: a 20-year low (ERP, 1998).

However, among all men, overall labor-force activity has deceased steadily over the last 25 years. In 1970, 86 percent of all men were working or looking for work; by 1993 this number had dropped to 78 percent of the workforce. The percent of men active in the labor market declines with decreasing educational attainment and is racially disparate as well. In 1993, when 72 percent of male high school dropouts were in the labor market, only 63 percent of black male high school dropouts—the group that has experienced the steepest wage declines—were active (Blank, 1998). Juhn (1999) emphasizes that while black men have fared well in this tight labor market in terms of a lowered unemployment rate, this beneficial effect has not extended to overall labor-force participation rates.

In contrast to the work activities of men, the labor-force participation of women has increased markedly in the past two decades, from 46 percent in 1975 to 59 percent in 1996 (Hayghe, 1997). This increase is most pronounced among more highly educated women who have also experienced the sharpest increase in wages, but even female high school dropouts show small increases in labor-force participation (Blank, 1998).

How These Trends May Affect Black/White Economic Differentials

Several explanations for the worsening economic condition of blacks[2] are attributed to the exogenous demand-side changes addressed here, including a shift from manufacturing to service jobs (Wilson, 1987, 1996; Bluestone and Harrison, 1982), which appears to have a disproportionately negative effect on the employment and earnings outcomes of less-educated workers in general and black male college graduates and high school dropouts in particular (Bound and Holzer, 1991; Bound and Freeman, 1992).[3]

Shifts within industries, attributable to technological changes, also appear to be reducing the number of medium-wage, medium-skill jobs for less-educated workers, further depressing the wages of blacks more than whites (Levy, Murnane, and Chen, 1993; Bound and Holzer, 1991).

The loss of low or medium-skill but medium-paid jobs (such as those created by the loss of unionized manufacturing jobs) has not only throw more people into competition for low-wage work, but has also reduced average wages for men who are not college graduates, especially black men, and raised inequality among male workers at all educational levels (Acs and Danziger, 1993; Bound and Holzer, 1991; Bound and Freeman, 1992; Danziger and Gottschalk, 1995). It has been shown that the occupational attainment of black men worsened from 1973 to 1989 relative to that of young whites with similar years of schooling.

Bound and Holzer (1991) surmise that most black-white earnings disparities are caused by the fact that blacks were in occupations with falling relative pay rather than the result of shifts from manufacturing to service jobs. Thus, there were more negative wage and employment effects from shifts *within* sectors, than shifts *between* sectors.

However, it was found that black men who were displaced from manufacturing fare more poorly than white men who were similarly situated (Bound and Freeman, 1992). Holzer (1995) suggests that barriers, such as discrimination, are keeping blacks from making transitions to other manufacturing jobs, or to jobs in other industries.

Perhaps the most compelling reason for growing black-white earnings and employment differentials is that there are growing economic returns to skills, and that blacks are concentrated in occupations with fewer skill requirements. However, it is important to realize that the increased returns to the college-educated are more the result of a decline in the real earnings of high school dropouts and high school graduates than an increase in earnings of college graduates (Gottschalk, 1997).

In addition, the growing earnings inequality of less- and more-skilled workers is only occurring in the United States, and to a lesser extent, in the United Kingdom, and not in other Organization of Economic Cooperation and Development (OECD) countries which have incurred similar technological changes and sectoral shifts. This may indicate that institutional factors may have resulted in a dramatic erosion of wages for the less-educated or those in certain jobs or sectors, more than a greater need for skills (Fortin and Lemieux, 1997; Gottschalk, 1997).

As they examine factors contributing to earnings inequality that lay outside the purview of simple supply and demand explanations, Fortin and Lemieux (1997) ask the question of why there is so much emphasis on male full-time workers and so little emphasis on the distibution of wages in the whole workforce (including part-time as well as full-time workers and the female workforce). They note that the main reason is data limitations. However, they stress that a focus on the full-time male workforce, divided by the easily quantifiable price and quantity of each education class, leads to an explanation that is most consistent with a supply and demand analysis. This may result in too much emphasis being placed on the high school/college differential as a compelling explanation for growing inequality among workers. This explanation may obscure the effects of less easily quantified factors, such as factors contributing to wage inequality, that they studied: the loss of the value of the minimum wage, the decline of unionization, and the effects of deregulation.

Here I attempt to address qualitatively factors relevant to the persistent economic gaps between black and white workers that are even less easy to measure than those pertinent to the decline of unionism or the value of the minimum wage. These include the effects of geographic segregation and employer discrimination. This focus is not to undermine the importance of skill-based explanations, which I also address, but to emphasize that the story of wage differences between black and white workers is not easily told through conventional quantitative analyses.

STUDY FINDINGS: WAGES AND RACE IN DETROIT

Table 4-1 presents average wages[4] at case-matched firms, classified by whether they are located in the city of Detroit or in the suburbs. Nearly all of the black-owned firms employed a greater percentage of black workers than their white-owned case matches. In addition, the higher the percentage of black workers at a firm, regardless of the race of its owner, the lower the average wages paid there. Most black-owned firms often paid substantially less than their white-owned counterparts.[5]

There are also locational differences in wages paid. White employers in the suburbs paid the highest wages; black-owned city firms tended to pay the least. White owners in the suburbs paid 22 percent more than white owners in the city ($11.23 versus $8.78/hour); white owners in the city paid 25 percent more than black owners in the suburbs ($8.78/hour versus $6.61); and black owners in the city paid the least of all ($6.28/hour), 5 percent less than suburban black-owned firms and 28 percent less than city white-owned firms.

Regression analysis was completed to determine whether black- and white-owned wage gaps are a function of the race of the owner or the percentage of black workers employed in the lower-wage firms. The results indicate that for the pairs of matched black-and white-owned firms, the wage gap between them increases as the gap in percentage of black employment increases.[6] The direction of this relationship is consistent with the hypothesis that larger percentages of black workers are associated with lower average wages.

A similar result is obtained from a multiple regression using the percent of black employees and a dummy variable to control for firm ownership. Because of the small sample size, neither of the results are statistically significant, but they suggest that the percentage of blacks employed, as well as the race of the owner, predicts wage levels.

Bates and Dunham have stated that supporting the creation of minority-owned businesses is one way to address deteriorating employment opportunities for urban blacks (1992). However, these findings suggest that such an approach may not eliminate earnings gaps between employed blacks and whites.

Table 4-1. Average Wages by Race of Employer and Employer Location

Black Firms	Av. Wage	White Firms	Av. Wage	Differ.	% Difference (black firms)
City Firms					
1. Cannon Ch. 97% black	$8.00	**Lackawan.** 0% black	$13.00	$5.00	38% less
2. Curve-All 100% black	$4.50	**Maybee** 80% black	$12.00 UAW	$7.50	41% less
3. Crowe Prod. 50% black	$8.50	**TopPoint** 75% black	$7.64 UAW	$0.86	4% more
4. Trail 100% black	$5.50	**Flamebest** 40% black	$7.00	$2.50	35% less
5 Sears Metals 90% black	$5.25	**Gratiot** 9% black	$6.50	$1.25	19% less
6. Satellite Fas. 30% black	$7.50	**Planet Pr.** 50% black	$8.70	$1.20	16% less
7. Morgan Stamp. 87% black	$6.00	**Dartmouth** 35% black	$7.00	$1.00	17% less
8. Silver 72% black	$5.50	**Sergeant** 50% black	$7.00	$1.50	21% less
9. CalOrange 100% black	$8.00	**Armstrong** 50% black	$10.20	$2.20	27.5% less
10. Woodward	No info.				
Average	**$6.28**		**$8.78**	**$2.50**	**28% less**
Suburban Firms		**USG** 0% black	$13.00		
11. Elizabeth 65% black	$6.10	**Mushroom** 5% black	Won't tell*		
12. Lionel 35% black UAW	$7.40	**Janis** 0% black	$11.50	$4.10	36% less
13. Twain 88% black	$6.33	**Mash Inc.** 3% black	$10.20 UAW	$3.87	38% less
Sub. Aver.	**$6.61**		**$11.23**	**$4.62**	**41% less**
Overall Aver.	**$6.36**		**$9.40**	**$3.04**	**32.3% less**

*Mushroom's respondents would only state that they start workers "at the community wage, between $8 and $9." I assume, then, that average wages would be substantially higher than those at Elizabeth.

WHY WAGES MAY BE LOWER IN BLACK-OWNED FIRMS AND IN FIRMS THAT EMPLOY A LARGE PERCENTAGE OF BLACK WORKERS

Researchers offering explanations for the employment and earnings gaps between white and black workers generally fall into two camps: those emphasizing demand-side changes at either the aggregate level (overall changing characteristics and locations of jobs), or the firm level (hiring and recruitment practices); and those emphasizing supply-side issues (changing work ethics, attitudes, skills, and demographic composition) among workers. However, boundaries between demand- and supply-side factors are often blurred: for instance, changing demand characteristics may induce changes in supply-side factors, as when falling wages offered by employers lead some workers to reject the labor market altogether. In any event, the direction of causation (i.e., does a growing pool of less-skilled workers depress employment and wage levels, or do low wage levels discourage workers?) is rarely clear.

The following chapters will address space- and skill-based arguments regarding black-white wage (and employment) gaps in detail, but first I would like to address how the characteristics of black-owned firms may affect wage levels, as well as present more general information about wages in the Detroit area.

A Situation of Unequal Competition Among Black-Owned Firms

The fact that black-owned firms pay lower wages than white-owned firms may be due to the fact that minority-owned and operated businesses have more trouble competing for Big Three contracts than white-owned firms. Four CEOs of minority-owned companies complained that the current competitive environment was leading the Big Three to diminish their Equal Employment Opportunity (EEO) policies. For example, the CEO of Twain Plastics states:

> . . . the minority programs don't stand, the only company out there with a true minority program of the Big Three is Chrysler. Chrysler, through their president, Mr. Lutz, has done some very aggressive things to try to bring minorities back into play, because he sensed that they were beginning to lose the minority suppliers. But when you start taking a look at what's really happening in the industry today, with the supplier reduction, well, you're killing off a lot of minority suppliers, and our situation here, you'd put another 50 black individuals out of work for some period of time.

The President of Morgan Stamping adds:

> Well, as the larger companies downsize, they're putting more black people into the unemployment group . . . as those same automotive companies look at their suppliers, and say who do we want in the future to do business with, they're cutting out smaller manufacturers, those that they say will not have the engineering support in the future that we're going to need, and a number of minority companies. And because of their sourcing decisions, those companies are also going out of business, and so there again you have minority companies dumping more people into that unemployment pool.

In other words, the Big Three are emphasizing cost-cutting above the goal of using minority suppliers.

Note that no information was gathered on the efficiency of the minority-owned firms or the quality of their products or differences in their production costs. Minority-owned businesses historically had less access to capital than white-owned firms, and although these barriers have eased in the last 25 years, levels of progress are said to have stalled (Bates and Dunham, 1992). Black-owned firms may be less efficient or they may face discrimination in access to capital, which would raise their production costs. For whatever reason, more minority-owned than white-owned businesses in this study consciously attempted to keep production costs lower than their competitors by offering lower wages to a predominantly African-American workforce.

The Context of Lower Wages in the City of Detroit

The lower wages offered, for the most part, by African-American-owned companies are in part due to the fact that, in this sample, wages for Detroit-based firms, whether they were white- or black-owned, are lower than wages offered at suburban white-owned firms. Only 3 of the 19 city firms offer starting wages over $8/hour, and only one started workers at a rate equal to or over what is considered the "community" wage in the suburbs: $9/hour.

Harry Holzer (1996), in his telephone survey of two thousand firms in the metropolitan Detroit area, found that average entry-level wages of all manufacturing firms in the city of Detroit are actually higher than those in the suburbs ($7.94 versus $7.57, respectively). In my sample, the average starting wages of black-owned firms in the city are also a bit higher than black-owned firms in the suburbs ($6.02 versus $5.59). However, the average starting wages of black-owned firms are 24 percent less than the average wage in Holzer's more representative sample. Starting wages offered by black-owned suburban firms in my sample are 25 percent less than the average starting wages in suburban manufacturing firms documented by Holzer.[7]

In the context of Holzer's findings, wages in my sample at white-owned suburban firms or firms with majority-white workforces are not unusually high, and wages at either white or black-owned firms with largely black workforces are very low. This may be the case because Holzer's findings do not address how the racial breakdown of workforces may affect wage rates and/or how the laws of supply and demand may differ for white and black workers (and employers who choose to hire either largely white or largely black workforces).

A Surplus of African-American Workers in the City of Detroit and a Shortage of Jobs

Both black and white employers who paid lower wages stated that there are relatively few low- or semi-skilled jobs available in the city of Detroit and a large number of both black and white workers seeking jobs. Employers noted that they received large numbers of applications for every opening, whether or not it had been advertised. In addition, many employers state that they could either lower wages or keep them low because they have a captive labor force at their disposal.

For example, representatives from two white-owned firms had cut wages in recent years. Armstrong Industries, a United Auto Workers (UAW) firm, dropped its starting wage in 6 years from $14/hour to $7.73/hour. Three other Detroit-based UAW firms in this study (Dartmouth, Maybee, and TopPoint Products) also have low starting wages, compared to a higher average wage. This may indicate that the union is more protective of the wage of its current members than it is of new hires.[8] In both firms with wage cuts, the change was made at the corporate level. Managers who chose to lower wages knew that, given the high unemployment rate in Detroit, enough workers could be found, even if workers accepting its lower entry-level wage were somewhat less skilled than previous new hires. The apparent trade-off between better skills and lower wages raises the question as to whether increased skills are needed in this industry (see chapter 6), or whether the worker-related cost savings associated with these cuts offset losses in skills and productivity.

At Armstrong Industries, which lowered wages by nearly 50 percent, the plant manager emphasized a job shortage/labor surplus in Detroit: "But again, there's a lot of people out there that are hurting for a job, so when you put up something saying $7.73 an hour, it's better than McDonald's so you know, I'll try that. . . . "

Armstrong Industries is now 50 percent black; it was 40 percent black before the institution of the latest wage cut. Workers man the same jobs at three different salary levels because of contracts that included a $3/hour wage cut 6 years before this interview was held, and another $3/hour cut 3 years after that. I do not know the racial composition of each tier, but the floor supervisor at Dartmouth Stamping gave this explanation as to why he thought African-American economic gains are eroding:

> I think I know the answer to that one. Well, it happened at XYZ Corporation on the east side of Detroit. . . . We were working there. . . . So what happened was, they were making like $9.50 an hour on the regular workforce, running the presses. And the manager says they can't afford it anymore. So they put a second tier in there. Everybody hired in from this date makes $5.50 an hour. And there it is. Your blacks are in your inner city, they're lower educated, the tier was put in, what happens? Who gets stuck with the $5 an hour? Five dollar an hour is the uneducated black man. There it is.

Dartmouth's supervisor indicates that he feels that the lower skills of the black workforce are determinants of lower wages. Yet, as the plant manager indicates, Armstrong Industries workers making $14/hour and those earning nearly half that stand next to one another completing the very same tasks. Two-tier wage structures have been introduced in a number of industries over the past 15 years even though lower wages may result in lower-skilled workers.

Other employers indicated that they could lower wages without upsetting their production because of a glut of available workers. TopPoint Products is a low-wage white-owned firm. Its $5.00/hour starting wage is 41 percent lower than its partially black-owned match, Crowe Products, which starts workers at $8.50/hour. Seventy-five percent of the people in TopPoint's sample job (production worker) are African American, while only 35 percent of the sample job workforce at Crowe Products is black. TopPoint's plant manager says job tenure averages "between 6 and 20 years," a result of the few employment alternatives for workers in the city: "In this location, they don't have really anyplace else that they can

get to that will provide the benefits and wage base that they're at now. . . .
I've had nobody leave to go to another facility, or for another job."

Finally, the white co-owner and floor supervisor of Sears Metals
says that their wages reflect the high unemployment in the area. Sears
Metals is a minority-owned business that is majority-owned by an
African-American woman. This company fabricates and repairs metal
racks used in the auto industry. Sears Metals starts at $4.75/hour, 14 per-
cent less than its white-owned match, Gratiot Welding, located one block
away from Sears Metals. The average wage at Sears is $5.25, 19 percent
less than Gratiot's $6.50 average. However Sears Metals is a union shop
(Teamsters) that offers very good benefits: full medical, partial optical,
five sick days per year; and one week's vacation after one year, two
weeks after two years. Gratiot offers no benefits at all. Thus, my focus on
money wages may exaggerate some of the differences in total compensa-
tion.

The supervisor at Sears exclaims: "You run across a lot of people
that are unemployed now, and wow!, when they were employed, they
might have made a fairly decent type wage, and because of the recession
and all the things that have happened, a lot of people are not able to pick
up on the same type of job they've had in prior years. . . . " He says that
they are able to attract people in spite of the wage because "we are a
company that employs people and allows people to make some type of
living, and we also offer benefits."

The white floor supervisor at minority co-owned Sears Metals states
(along with several other respondents) that he believed that black workers work for lower wages than white workers:

> I find that nine times out of ten that the blacks seem to be more eager to
> go to work for less money. They're not afraid to work, either. . . . I've
> had many, many black guys who could work, you couldn't put any
> other race next to them and keep up with them. Very hard-working peo-
> ple. . . . I just think that the majority of them have had a pretty tough
> life. I mean, I've worked hard, I mean, I don't care about the racial
> thing, I mean, I've got white guys out here that have been with me for
> just as long as the black guys that are just as hard of workers. But, in
> the past 5 years, I think the black people that I have hired, it seems like
> they want to work harder than the whites I've seen.

Even when reviewed in a national context of deteriorating job opportunities and wages for low-skilled workers, the decline of job opportunities

and wages in the city of Detroit has been particularly pronounced. In this context, it is apparent that many workers will seek and keep often arduous jobs in spite of the low wages paid. Employers in several other firms say that they are able to maintain low wages without incurring increased turnover.

For example, Cannon Chemical is a minority-owned firm where wages are low, but the CEO reports no attitude or turnover problems. Cannon Chemical offers starting wages that are substantially below those of its white-owned match, Lackawanna Chemical ($6.50 versus $10.00, or 35 percent); there is also a 38 percent average wage gap ($8.00 versus $13.00), and benefits for the two firms are similar. Cannon Chemical's workforce in the sample job of production worker is nearly 100 percent African American while Lackawanna Chemical's is 100 percent white. Both firms indicate few problems with worker attitude or turnover.

Yet most of the black employers in both the city and the suburbs, as well as city white employers who offer lower wages, incur high turnover. Nine of the 12 low-paying firms in the sample find it more profitable to keep their wages low at the expense of having an applicant base with better worker morale and loyalty, and lower turnover.[9]

For example, the production manager at Armstrong Industries believes his firm's wage cut has made a difference in both production and profitability. The fact that workers are performing identical jobs alongside each other at different wage levels has been particularly bad for worker morale: "[A]fter they get their time in like that, why am I working here making $7.73 an hour doing this, and this guy standing right next to me is making $12, $13 an hour doing the exact same thing, I should get as much as that. Well, when you hired in you knew what the score was but then you needed the job real bad, but now you're here and you've got your time, gee, you don't want to do it like that. I've heard that, you know, I'm working as hard as $7.73 will allow me. Well, we don't keep people like that around too often, with an attitude. But the attitude is there."

Most low-wage employers spoke of their workers' willingness to quit their jobs at a moment's notice. All but 3 respondents out of the 12 firms that pay low wages stressed that workers voluntarily quit for jobs with better wages even if no benefits are offered. Low-paying firms tolerate high turnover and thereby save benefits that kick in only after a probation period that may last as long as one year, as well as worker development costs (however, they incur higher costs of hiring). Firm managers and owners will do this (such as Armstrong Industries and Curve-All) even if some members of management feel that the organization would be better served by higher wages and lower turnover.

The director of a program designed to train auto workers in new skills and technology suggests that this trend to substitute worker loyalty and skills for low wages is widespread. He states that, on the whole, the auto industry puts no time and money into training low-skilled workers:

> . . . they're more willing to train but they train the highly skilled. And that's why our customized training is to the skilled trades person and up, we rarely get, we always have employers talk about coming in and doing a basic skills class for their hourly, unskilled workforce, but they never do it. They talk about it."

With regard to turnover, he continued:

> They allow the turnover, that's right. And they don't have, there is no career path. We're basically competing on the world market in terms of low wage, low skills, rather than anything else. I mean the decision's been made, and it has been for a long time here. . . . We developed an education system that was able to take people along the high-skills track, but the prospective business has been that short-term profit deal always dominates, so as result, the biggest return was always staying on that short rip-off. And that's what they did to us, that's what we've got. That's where we compete, so most of the jobs you're talking about in manufacturing are going to stay on the low end.

NOTES

[1]Bound and Freeman (1992) note that disparities between blacks and whites (at least in employment) again began widening in the 1970s, before the actions of Reagan and Bush substantially weakened the affirmative action gains made in earlier years.

[2]Before I describe this literature in more detail, it should be noted that almost all the cited studies focus on young black men. However, several papers have been written recently that address wage and employment disparities between black and white women. These studies confirm that growing wage and employment gaps between blacks and whites are not gendered phenomena; growing racially based economic gaps among women are also documented, though differ-

ences are not as great among white and black young women as they are among black and white young men.

[3]For general reviews on both supply- and demand-side explanations for the worsening condition of black men in the labor market, see Moss and Tilly, 1991a, and Holzer, 1995.

[4]Detailed wage data is presented in Appendix A. Average wages are for the determined "sample" job: in most cases I focused on the same sample job when I later completed interviews at the white-owned case matches. Although starting wages may be the most sensitive to current market conditions, I have elected to focus here on "average" wages in order to give a sense of whether workers have opportunity to advance themselves financially within their job category—thus giving a better indication of whether a job is especially "dead end," whether or not promotional opportunities are present.

[5]This finding is in concurrence with that of Hirsch and Schumacher (1992), who found that wages for both white and black workers were significantly lower in industries, regions, or occupations with a high proportion of blacks.

[6]Equations are presented in Appendix B.

[7]However, the standard deviation for city wages was greater than those for suburban wages ($3.39 versus $3.10).

[8]Note that Maybee's average wage in the sample job is $12.00; a cut in starting wages may also have occurred at this firm. Since cuts in wages have received little play in the black-white employment gap literature, questions relating to this issue in my instrument were unfortunately excluded.

[9]These include 4 white-owned firms (Armstrong Industries, Dartmouth, Maybee, and TopPoint Products) and 5 black-owned firms (Curve-All, Twain, Elizabeth, Trail, and Sears Metals).

CHAPTER 5

Wages and Space

Given that wages paid for entry-level work in the auto-supply industry appear to be higher in the suburbs than in the city—which may reflect a labor surplus in the city of Detroit— why don't city workers seek better-paying jobs in the suburbs? Are there spatial impediments for African-American workers either to finding out about job opportunities in the suburbs or traveling there to search for or attend work? Many authors have addressed the issue of spatial barriers to employment as expressed by the theory of spatial mismatch.

The theory of spatial mismatch posits that many urban African Americans are impeded from making locational adjustments to a changing labor market through the variable of space. Theorists agree that both jobs and populations have been becoming more decentralized through the years, but black populations, because of housing discrimination, have not been able to move to suburban areas in the same numbers or with the same degree of dispersion as whites. One effect of spatial mismatch is that the increased costs of commuting, along with insufficient labor market information, affects the labor market outcomes of blacks.[1]

Continued physical isolation from jobs, in the face of continued decentralization of populations and industries, further decreases the probability that blacks can either obtain information about work, inexpensively search for it, or commute to it when found. This, in turn, decreases the likelihood of affording suburban housing—therefore blacks experience multiple "feedback effects" from the initial discriminatory acts in housing markets.

The early literature on spatial mismatch proposes increasing access to jobs for black urban residents through the provision of better transportation to suburban jobs. The problem with this notion is that although the transportation system offers mobility, which delivers access over space, the distance between minority urban populations and suburban jobs was not created through chance: it is one of the tangible manifestations of larger institutional and social factors. It is not an objective notion of "space" that constrains access but larger social forces, such as negative racial attitudes, expressed through the practices of firms and other institutions, that work through spatial variables.

Therefore, distance *in itself* cannot be the only cause of such economic gaps between whites and blacks. Further testimony to this notion is provided by black-owned and some white-owned suburban firms in this sample which have recruited a high number of minority workers. The white-owned organizations either chose or were forced to adhere to strict affirmative action guidelines.[2] Although transportation concerns are pressing for many urban residents, antidiscriminatory employer attitudes and practices also have an effect.

To provide a context for this argument, I review the principal assumptions and methodological limitations of spatial mismatch theory. I use the employer interviews to present two issues not explored in the spatial mismatch literature: harassment of nonresident African-American workers by the suburban police and local residents and discriminatory hiring practices. I follow this with employer perceptions about transportation problems among their urban workforce. I then compare the hiring practices of case-matched black- and white-owned suburban firms, and suggest that black-owned firms are far more likely to use recruiting methods that lead to a larger pool of black applicants than white-owned firms.

I also found that suburban firms that were under affirmative action pressure hired a larger number of black urban workers. These firms hired higher percentages of African Americans for better-paid jobs because of strict EEO programs implemented to adhere to federal and state legislative mandates (at least in two cases) or because of a judgment resulting from an antidiscrimination lawsuit (in one case). Even though these employers drew their African-American workers primarily from the city of Detroit, none reported that workers had transportation difficulties in applying for jobs, or in reaching their jobs once they were hired.

SPATIAL MISMATCH THEORY

Until the mid-1980s empirical evidence provided equivocal support for a theory of spatial mismatch. This was due to conceptual and resultant methodological problems that may have skewed or understated the problem. These problems include an interrelationship of earnings and place of residence, which complicate attempts to gauge distance effects. Holzer (1991) notes that the textbook model of residential choice begins with the assumption that employment is fixed in the central city and that people are free to choose their residential locations throughout the metropolitan area; this model also assumes that people make a trade-off between higher housing prices in the central city and longer commute distances from the suburbs. Therefore, higher-income people should be found in both the city and the suburbs and wages should be higher for those living further from their places of employment to compensate for longer commutes.

However, residential and industrial decision-making is far more complicated than that. Racial considerations are part of residential choice (Farley, 1979), workplaces are now suburbanized, and city life is often considered to be a disamenity. Distance and commute times may rise either when a poorer central-city resident is commuting to a suburban location, or when a wealthier individual is seeking to reside in an area far from commercial enterprises. However, distance from employment does tend to rise with income, since commuting costs at some point prohibit far commutes for the poorer worker. The sole use of distance to work as a measure of mismatch is misleading, since people with the highest incomes most often have the longest commutes.

Another methodological problem of early studies is selective migration, which fails to take into consideration that while the majority of suburban migrants are white, blacks have also been slowly suburbanizing. Therefore, the divergences we later see in city and suburban black employment rates, wages, and income may be due to the selective migration of more employable blacks to the suburbs. The better earnings and employment rates of suburban blacks are less a result of their physical proximity to jobs and more a reflection of greater human capital. Jencks and Mayer (1989) have stated that the failure to take selective migration into account is the "single most important reason why we have learned so little about this subject in the two decades since Kain first advanced the spatial mismatch hypothesis" (p. 220).

Findings of Early Studies

The notion of spatial mismatch was first presented by John Kain in 1968. He related the fractions of black employment in various neighborhoods in Detroit and Cleveland to their residential distribution across these neighborhoods, as well as their distance to the central business district (CBD). Kain noted that the fraction of black employment related positively to the distribution of residences and negatively to the average distance to the CBD. He infers that residential integration (where blacks are dispersed in the same fashion as whites throughout the city) would increase black employment from 3 to 8 percent (Kain, 1968).

Holzer notes that Mooney, using 1960 data, focused on measures of job suburbanization to avoid the problem of unobserved personal characteristics of populations. He found that the greater the proportion of jobs in selected industries that were located in the suburbs, the lower the employment rates of inner-city blacks, controlling for the fraction of employed city blacks who work in the suburbs. Holzer further states that Harrison, in a 1972 study, used measures of residential suburbanization to determine the employment effects of the decentralization of jobs and the concentration of blacks in inner cities. He found no difference in employment or earnings between black and white residents of city and suburban areas (cited in Holzer, 1991). A problem with this study is that, as Massey and Denton (1988) have documented, blacks are not widely dispersed in the suburbs, and may cluster quite close to city borders. This study does not control for distance to jobs.

Holzer (1991) lists additional problems with these early studies, including their focus on males. A focus on employed male household heads excludes individuals with severe employment problems and produces downward biases in estimated racial differences, especially in annual earnings. Holzer notes a problem related to the inability to determine how close black suburban residents are to suburban jobs, for even if employers are leaving heavily black neighborhoods, their exact locations may or may not be far from the borders of these neighborhoods. Measures of residential or job decentralization, determined solely by city or suburban location, give little insight into job access for black residents.

Later Findings

David Ellwood's 1986 study of the effects of neighborhood distance from commercial centers on black and white employment probabilities in Chicago departs from these earlier efforts in several ways. He attempts to mitigate selection effects by focusing on youth (although it can be argued that the job-determined locational choices of their parents affect results). He also incorporates measures of travel times into his equations, as well as measures of distance.

Overall, Ellwood found that job proximity exerts a small but statistically reliable influence on teenage employment rates: males between the ages of 16 and 21 were more likely to be working if they lived in neighborhoods with a lot of nearby jobs (thereby emphasizing the effects of the costs of car ownership and public transportation on low-earning youth).

These findings led Ellwood to write that it is race, not space that adversely influences the employment outcomes of black youth. Another interpretation of his findings may be that Chicago has an unusually efficient public transportation system that would significantly improve access, as measured in travel times, to jobs outside the considered neighborhood.

Ihlanfeldt and Sjoquist (1990) looked at the cities of Los Angeles and Chicago and found large distance effects on the employment of black youth, but not on the employment of white youth, the latter who seem more able to overcome obstacles to employment in these cities. There were some operational differences between their and Ellwood's specifications, but the fact that their results for Chicago are different than Ellwood's is in keeping with the notion extended by Holzer (1991) and Jencks and Mayer (1989) that the effects of spatial mismatch have increased since the 1970s. Results may also reflect the fact that these cities have experienced further out-migration and loss of industry in recent years, coupled with a lower than average rate of black suburbanization. In all, these studies demonstrate that there are strong differences across metropolitan areas in the effects of spatial mismatch.

In 1992, Holzer, Ihlanfeldt, and Sjoquist found that access to cars significantly increased the distances over which people will search for work, and also raised wages and probabilities for employment. The relatively low car ownership among inner-city blacks seems to contribute to their lower earnings and employment (of course, the causal direction of this relationship is unclear). The greater suburbanization of employment in metropolitan areas resulted in an increase in search and commuting costs that may affect both search and work behavior of urban blacks. Black youth were found to travel shorter distances to search for work; their travel times for these searches, however, were far longer than those of whites searching over similar distances. For example, the time spent per mile was 46 percent higher for black males and 55 percent higher for black females, which points to the increased costs associated with the use of public transportation. As a result, blacks searched for jobs over shorter distances than whites, but attempted to compensate for this disadvantage by searching longer and using more search methods than whites.

Zax and Kain (1991) used a case-study methodology to analyze responses over time by white and black workers to the relocation of a single large firm from central-city Detroit to a suburban location in Dearborn. This study relied on longitudinal data and examines 8 years of employment records, including new hires, for an eight hundred person firm in the service industry located in Detroit's CBD. During the 4th year, the firm moved to Dearborn. The authors then looked at the effects of the relocation on worker's moves, quits, and commuting adjustments.

Their results showed strong evidence that residential segregation constrained blacks' options in adjusting to the relocation of the firm. While all workers make trade-offs between income and commuting (workers generally commute longer for better-paying jobs), black workers appeared not to be as able to make trade-offs as easily as white workers. Zax and Kain found a stronger relationship between commuting and income for whites than for blacks; blacks were being forced to commute to jobs to which whites being paid similar wages would not.

In addition to commuting, they noted that changing residence and quitting are also readjustment mechanisms for spatial mismatch, and it is expected that these will be traded off with one another. Blacks were found to be more constrained than whites in using these options for resolving the spatial disruption that the firm's move caused. Moves and quits were directly substitutable reactions to the relocation for whites, but this was not the case for blacks.

Fernandez (1991) studied the effect of one Milwaukee firm's move from the city to the suburbs on the wages and employment of black and white workers. He improved on the methodology of Zax and Kain in several ways. He knew that this firm's decision to relocate was made exogenous to racial considerations, and he could directly examine the income and personal characteristics of people responding to the move with another move, thus controlling for selection effects.

Fernandez focused on distance and travel times, and using a model of time valuation, estimated the costs of commuting time in monetary terms for minorities and nonminorities. He found that minorities lived much closer to the CBD plant (7 miles on average) than whites (19 miles on average). White salaried workers lived even further than white hourly workers (25.68 versus 18.78 miles). Because of residential segregation, there was much greater variation in distances for whites than for blacks. Black and Hispanic workers lived in communities with large concentrations of their own groups, whereas white residences are much more spatially diverse (this was also found to be the case by Massey and Denton in their 1989 study).

Fernandez concludes that while the suburbanization of employment is growing rapidly, the suburbanization of minorities is not. Plant suburbanization does indeed produce mismatches between worker's residences and jobs, and these are most severe for minorities. He views this paper as a "microcosm of what is at stake in spatial mismatch hypothesis" (p. 25). In contrast to the findings of Holzer, Ihlanfeldt, and Sjoquist, Fernandez sees car ownership as doing little to undo the deleterious effects of firm moves on minorities and women.

Interview studies

Moss and Tilly's interview (1991b) evidence supports elements of the spatial mismatch hypothesis, but also presents a more complex picture than theory has, to this point, allowed. Manufacturers who chose suburban locations to obtain cheap land fit the model well, but other patterns—such as insurance companies following target white workforce to suburbs; and companies remaining downtown, refusing to hire blacks, and providing efficiency wages to draw white commuters; as well as the fact that retailers have also left the city to follow their customer base; and the fact that customer locational preferences are an issue for some manufacturers—all indicate that it will take far more than transportation programs (e.g., see Hughes, 1991) to offset locational effects.

Moss and Tilly, during their interviews of employers in Detroit and Los Angeles, pursued two lines of questioning pertinent to firm locational decision-making. They first asked about the history of the firm and reasons for past and contemplated moves, and second, asked opinions on why businesses have left the central city. Their data show traces of three fairly well-known locational shifts to suburbs: insurance, manufacturing, and retail. Insurance companies moved to be closer to a targeted workforce of white, English-speaking women (the one interviewed insurance company that remained in the city offers higher wage levels to attract a higher-quality inner-city workforce). Retail locations were also determined by the location of a largely white customer base.

Moss and Tilly found that manufacturing firms present a more varied picture. Manufacturers are more likely to cite nonlabor-related reasons for relocation—particularly land costs and availability. However, when manufacturing firms that planned to leave the city were asked the reasons for their move, they were likely to cite taxes, congestion, crime, and "image" issues. Moss and Tilly were convinced that in the midst of this, some auto manufacturers were clearly responding to same kind of target workforce signals as insurers. For instance, in Detroit many small manufacturers joined white flight to the suburbs following the '67 riot. One manager, when asked why businesses have left Detroit, stated: "[I]ts bad image and workforce quality, it's hard to get people to come there . . . everyone else was expanding and moving out here [the suburbs]. It's hard to get workers to come into city."

On the other hand, a city location does not ensure accessibility to potential black workers. A Detroit employer interviewed by Moss and Tilly asserted that the location of the firm did not scare off customers or potential employees. However, he admitted to having an all-white workforce.

Moss and Tilly also write that locational effects form a feedback pattern: once patterns of economic decline and racial concentration have set in urban areas, still other residents and businesses will choose to relocate. This pattern is all too evident in Detroit, where white residents and businesses have virtually abandoned the city.

Employment Audit Studies

The 1988 Urban Institute employment audit study, which used white and black matched pairs to investigate the incidence and extent of racial discrimination in hiring, found no difference in outcomes for white and black partners in suburban versus city firms, which may be a result of the fact that all jobs that the auditors responded to were listed in the *Washington Post,* a metropolitan newspaper. The implication is that if an employer is adverse to hiring blacks, they would target their recruiting efforts to white publications/agencies/neighborhoods—which is what Kirschenman and Neckerman found in 1989 (Kirschenman and Neckerman, 1991b).

However, another audit study conducted in 1988 by the Fair Employment Council auditors found substantial differences in treatment and outcomes toward black applicants from suburban firms compared to city firms (they used employment agencies and industrial listings as sources):

black-white tests showed an 18.9 percent rate of discrimination in the District of Columbia, and a 37.2 percent rate in its two surrounding suburban areas.

Conclusion: The Literature

Although studies completed before 1986 provide only equivocal support for a spatial mismatch hypothesis, later studies provide strong evidence for a spatial mismatch between black workers and suburban jobs. However, as audit studies have suggested, what might be seen as the effects of geographic distance on the wages and employment probabilities of urban youth in these studies may in part be a proxy for other factors, including firm-level locational decisions and hiring and recruitment methods that are specifically implemented to avoid contact with blacks.

Ihlanfeldt (1997) has recently published a paper reviewing the findings of spatial mismatch studies of the 1990s noting that taken as a whole there is clear evidence that spatial mismatch harms African Americans as a group, and particularly negatively affects the employment outcomes of young adults and women. There is also evidence that the effects of spatial mismatch have grown over time (cited in Moss and Tilly, 1998).

Employer Interview Findings: Spatial Factors

Many researchers have treated employer locational decision-making as if it were independent of racial considerations. As noted, recent evidence from interview and audit studies has indicated that employers may move to avoid black populations and keep their workforces white. Therefore, firm-level practices, such as locational decisions that reflect a desire to maintain distance from black neighborhoods and/or workers, as well as recruitment and hiring practices that adversely affect blacks, should both be considered when methodologically assessing the problem of spatial mismatch and when formulating policies to ameliorate its effects.

As can be seen from historical and recent evidence, the desire of whites to preserve distance from black populations is often a key factor in locational decisions on the part of white residential populations and firms, a fact which challenges the assumption that merely removing physical barriers to places of employment would improve the labor market outcomes of blacks.

My study findings are presented here to give a better idea of how historical social and institutional factors came together in the Detroit metropolitan area in a way that resulted in a particularly extreme condition of racial residential and employment segregation: the condition that supports the relevance of the theory of spatial mismatch.

Very little attention has been paid to the role of employer discrimination in spatial mismatch theory. Employer practices have only been briefly introduced into the debate through the findings of Moss and Tilly, as well as through findings of Harry Holzer, who found that suburban employers had far larger ratios of black applicants to black hires than city employers (1995). Moss and Tilly's finding that employers may move to the suburbs to follow a target white workforce and/or escape hiring African Americans supports the experience of an official I interviewed, Dave Sanders of the Southeast Michigan Council of Governments (SEMCOG), who attempted to institute a van service providing transportation for low-wage city workers to the suburbs. There was one problem—they could not get enough employers to participate. When asked why, most said they didn't want black workers, stating: "[W]hy do you think we moved out here?"

Respondents' Perceptions about the Treatment of African Americans in Detroit's Suburbs

The long history and often violent reaction of whites to the presence of African Americans in Detroit presented is presented in chapter 2 to give a context and an explanation for the seeming inability of urban blacks either to live or work in suburbs with better-paying jobs. Unfortunately, this heritage of intolerance continues. Of 22 African-American respondents interviewed for this study, 4 recounted recent incidences of racial harassment without having been asked a formal question pertinent to this topic.[3] I've also included the comments of white auto-parts suppliers, as well respondents interviewed as part of the MCSUI effort, who offered additional insight into what black workers experience when traveling in the suburbs.

The director of operations at Curve-All felt that it was difficult for the workers he so disparaged to move out of the city:

> I had a welding supplier that Chrysler called me and they needed some parts, and I needed some parts from his place. So I found out where he lived, and I went over to his house, and no sooner than I went up and knocked on the door, I mean there was police from everywhere. And it

was just basically because someone saw me, and knew that I did not belong in that area.

This area is West Bloomfield, an upper-middle-class suburb of Detroit. The director stated that the person to whom he was delivering parts actually had to escort him from his home to his car, and that:

> to be honest with you, I felt slightly uncomfortable, going uninvited. . . . The guy that owned the welding company told me that one of his neighbors saw me, called the police right away. And I could have been going over to visit. But I guess he must not have black people that come to his house.

He thought the worst places for him to visit as a black man were "probably Warren, out in like Shelby Township, out there at 26 Mile Road, Sterling Heights, that area out in there," which, as described in chapter 3, is the Groesbeck Corridor, where most of the auto-supply shops of the metropolitan area are located. He also noted how few blacks work there: "I had a guy, a Jewish fellow that owned the welding company, that I went out to his house, and he always told me, he goes, oh, man, I'm over here in Warren, I get some pretty good workers over here. But you'd go in the shop, there'd only be one or two minorities."

‑ This respondent described other neighborhoods where African Americans are hassled as "any of them that you don't belong in." He said that Southfield (an integrated northwest suburb immediately north of the city of Detroit) is the only suburb that he feels comfortable in. He did not say that discrimination has gotten worse in recent years, but he noted that: "I'll put it like this, I don't think it's gotten better."

The black president of Woodward Gas thinks there is more racial discrimination in blue-collar suburbs than in upper-income suburbs:

> The threat is I can move to West Bloomfield, and my property would be an acre and Henry Ford's property would be an acre and we'd never have to see each other. But if I moved to Livonia (a blue-collar western suburb), then we're next door to each other and it's closer. So I've found that the higher you are on an economic scale, the less threat a black person is to you. In Livonia, or Warren, Warren is one step up from Detroit, supposedly. Actually, economically, it isn't, but mentally it is. I live in Warren versus Detroit, but I'm still working at Chrysler on the assembly line, right next to Frank Johnson who lives in Detroit,

on the assembly line, so Frank Johnson's kid and my kid graduate from high school and they're vying for the same job. And Frank Johnson's kid may be an A student and mine may be a C student, so how do I ensure that my kid gets the job? I've got to put these artificial barriers, and so the guy sitting there perpetuates that, or people hire their friends.

However, he told me he experienced what he perceived to be racial discrimination four months prior to the interview:

I was going to lease a condo in West Bloomfield, well, back up. Same leasing, rental company, I was going to lease a condo in Southfield, I was approved in September. December, I decided, I canceled the one in Southfield and decided to move to West Bloomfield, and I was denied for credit. Now, my credit went bad between September and December? And I'm thinking about suing cause I think that if I placed that case, if I was qualified to move in Southfield in September, there's no way in hell I'm not qualified to move in West Bloomfield in December. Other than I may have been the first black family in that complex. So, yeah, it's out there, and it's people deciding where you're going to live, where you're going to get your mortgage, where you're going to get your bank loan, if we're going to give you the bank loan, if you're making too much money, what contract you're going to get. . . .

The floor supervisor at Curve-All was born and raised in Kentucky, and appears to have a certain comfort level with segregation. He says he thought that he had less problems in the suburbs than other African-American people he knows because of his manner:

I've been out to the Sterling Heights plant, I've been to the Dearborn plant, the Woodhaven plant, and I've been to a plants in Ohio, two of those, the two plants. I haven't had no problems. Other people that have been from here said they went to the plants, and you know, they was prejudiced, they were giving them a hard time, but nobody ever gave me a problem. I don't know if it's because I don't say nothing to them, I'll just go in and ask what's wrong, I'll do what I have to, and I go ahead and leave. I don't know why they had problems, I don't know.

However, when he was in Dearborn for social reasons, he was pulled over by police twice. One incident was when he went to a club with a white co-worker:

> I was on, out there in Dearborn, and we was going to, we went out to a club. Me and her, two more, a girl and another guy, they kept asking me to come out, wanted me to come out with them, and this was for like about three months, they kept asking me to go out with them. So I decided one day to go, and it was out there in Dearborn, at Frankie's, they're not open now. So I went in there, kind of nervous.

This supervisor stated that he usually feels nervous when he is out in Dearborn (a community set up by Henry Ford as a white enclave for himself and his workforce—it has few black residents to this day).[4] However, Dearborn now has the largest Arab-American population in the state, with much racial tension between this group and white residents:

> Well, it was nervous cause I went in and I saw just pretty much a whole lot of white folks, it like clicked, you know. But after I got in there I saw, you know, a few black folks in there, so then I kind of cooled out. Plus they looked at me funny when I walked in the door, that didn't help. So I took her back home. . . . It was like about four o'clock in the morning when we left that place, and I took her home, I dropped her off, and when I was coming back out, police car pulled me over. And he asked me did I see a truck go down the street? And I told him, I wasn't paying attention. So he asked me some more questions, you know, this kind of stuff, and he let me go. And I just knew, just cause I was in that neighborhood.

He also related other workers he knew have been pulled over in Warren and Sterling Heights for "for going to work on time." He also noted that he "was like out in Inkster, and he (a police officer) didn't have no reason to pull me over, he just pulled me over cause I was pretty much in a car, cause I was in a sports car . . . they pulled me over when I was on Sheldon Road, he pulled me over because I had my fog lights on. And I'm looking at people passing me with their fog lights on, so. . . . Well, it's funny, they never harass me or nothing, they just pull me over just to be pulling me over, I guess."

The president of Twain Plastics moved from Warren to his current location in Troy (which is about 8 miles farther north of the city than the border suburb of Warren) because "it would probably have been more difficult to attract the workforce that I want (his entry-level workforce is 98 percent black). Warren is an extremely racist area. . . . Well, it's much worse than Troy . . . it's all redneck."

White Employer's Stories about Discrimination in the Suburbs of Detroit

The floor supervisor at Dartmouth Stamping in Detroit spoke about what he considered to be his own boss's racial discrimination (this supervisor also admitted to not feeling comfortable if his workforce is more than 35 percent black, or "50 percent tops"). However, he emphasized that he believed the situation for blacks is worse in the Groesbeck Corridor than it is in his city firm:

> They're (black workers) not going to go to a suburb to try to find a job, they'll be lucky to make it there to look. They'll pull them over because it's a black man in Roseville. "What are you doing here, boy?" . . . I used to work in Madison Heights (a northern part of the Groesbeck Corridor), I brought people with me to Madison Heights, black people, good people. People will make them a villain over the way they walk. They would put them in jail. I mean, and I knew that was total racialism [*sic*]. And they don't even want to go through there. I know a lot of black people go around Dearborn. . . . So they sure wouldn't go look for a job there, right? If they're afraid to drive through the streets. Same with Madison Heights. Small little community, you know. It's the truth, though . . . (it's) very real.

He further comments on the probability of a black person being pulled over by the police:

> Oh, that's real high. They're watched, they're followed. Like I said, like in Madison Heights, I took black people out there and I had jobs, and they're always harassed.

This supervisor also mentioned how the constant pulling over of cars driven by blacks by the suburban police then affects their ability to maintain the costs of car ownership—constant tickets raise the cost of already-high city insurance rates. He concludes: "Do you live in Detroit? Oh, that'll be another $50 a month."

TRANSPORTATION OBSTACLES

As described in the spatial mismatch literature, black workers do face transportation obstacles beyond that of police harassment. These include the comparatively high cost of car ownership for residents of the city of Detroit, and an especially poor public transportation system. Both the literature on spatial mismatch and interview findings leave little doubt that the increased costs of car ownership, coupled with an inadequate transportation system, affect job search behavior and worker timeliness once a job is obtained. However, it is interesting to find that these problems do not seem to deter large groups of African Americans from either applying to or working in suburban firms in this and the MCSUI sample who have employers willing to interview and hire them—even if these jobs do not offer an adjustment of wages to compensate for increased commutation costs.

The Increased Cost of Car Ownership

As the floor supervisor at Dartmouth mentioned, the cost of car ownership is increased for city residents by significantly higher insurance rates. A downtown retailer interviewed as part of the MCSUI effort said of African-American city residents "they can't afford the basic operating expenses of car ownership. The emissions test alone is $50." And, "when you're talking to a person who is making minimum wage, $50 is a lot of money." In addition, several MCSUI employers also stated that the Michigan insurance companies redline. One Detroit manufacturer noted that car insurance costs in Detroit are "terrible, just terrible," he says that his 23-year-old son's insurance was $2,000 a year in Detroit; while in North Carolina, it is $600. He also mentions that a woman in the office moved out of Detroit to the suburbs, and "her insurance dropped from $1,200 to $800."

Other MCSUI employers described institutional and educational barriers to car ownership. A personnel officer in a security firm on the border of Detroit told me that city schools have stopped offering driver education. A city retailer also lamented the lack of education pertinent to car ownership: "How do you get a driver's license, how do you get insurance for a car, how do you buy a car, how do you become mobile?"

Poor Public Transportation Options

Seven respondents from the 18 city case-matched firms thought that poor public transportation options caused problems in their workers' ability either to get to work in a timely fashion or to retain their jobs (and, as presented below, a few of these employers are skeptical about their workers' transportation-related excuses).

In contrast, respondents from the MCSUI sample were more apt to describe the deficiencies of the Metropolitan Detroit transportation system. The Metropolitan Detroit bus system is inefficiently divided into two separately owned and barely solvent services: one in the city and the other servicing the rest of the metro region; recent efforts to merge these systems failed primarily because of the opposition of suburban politicians. In addition, there is no commuter train service at all.

It is possible that the differences between the MCSUI respondents and those from this study may reflect the fact that so few of the MCSUI sample firms were located in the city. Poor public transportation has a long history in Motor City, where car ownership has always been encouraged, partially through car companies' lobbying efforts that resulted in the failure to provide either efficient or low-cost public alternatives (Jackson, 1985).

In all, city respondents who complained about the public transportation system described it as inefficient, costly, and having far fewer routes than required to bring a city-based population adequately to jobs in the suburbs.

Employer Views about Public Transportation

The plant manager of TopPoint Products says that 75 percent of the African Americans he employs (the firm is 75 percent black) rely on public transportation to get to work, and that this reliance

> does tend to lead to absenteeism, and with the public transportation it depends on how it's running . . . with the public transportation, the weather's a factor. A lot of them do arrange for rides for people that do work here, but if that individual decides not to come in that day, I've got 8 hours left out of my 16, they're up a creek at that point, by the time they realize that, public transportation's come and gone, and it's difficult if they're not in walking distance. There's some of them that, they'll walk, two or three miles.

African-American workers walking long distances to work in often inclement weather was noted by several other respondents. The president of Cannon Chemical noted that he has a worker who walks every day, winter, summer, spring, he walks . . . [he] works at night, we try not to give him late hours in the winter time because he doesn't have a car. He's a fairly new employee and his goal is to get one once he's gotten the chance to save some money but he also has a wife and 4 kids, and how much can you save when you've got a wife and 4 kids? But he's an excellent worker. So, because of that, there's a buddy system in which they try to make certain that they transport him home at night.

This respondent, like many employers with largely black workforces, tried to ensure that employees

kind of look out for each other, it's not an automatic thing. But were they not to do it I would urge them to do so, and I've made it very clear I don't want him working late. So I set my own personal policy, if I go back there at seven o'clock in the winter time, I'll make certain that someone understands that it is my expectation they're gonna take care of him in a way that gets him home without walking that late at night. They're not responsible for him, I'm not saying that, but I'd want them to have that level of concern.

He also notes that workers make it to work in spite of the limitations of public transportation, even if this poses hardships:

We have a number of people we see walking in from Oakman Boulevard when they come in the morning because they do take the bus, and their commitment is to be here, and to pay whatever the price is to be here, whether it's getting up at five o'clock in the morning and taking the bus or whatever.

Like the president of Cannon, the white supervisor at black-owned Crowe Products notes that he'll sometimes go out of his way to make sure workers can overcome the impediments caused by poor transportation: "Yes, some people do have trouble getting here. They don't have adequate transportation, there is really nothing but bus service in Detroit, which is terrible." When asked whether he views whites and blacks as having equal transportation problems, he replies:

No, seems like more of the white guys have newer cars and that. For some reason the black guys have older cars. But it's also true of the younger fellows too, they have older cars and problems with transportation. . . . Now if their car breaks down, you're in trouble . . . then we send the maintenance man out in a pick-up truck to load them up. . . . Well, yes, it's been rare, but it has happened. It's usually right in the immediate area, where the guy got off the freeway and the car died or something, it wasn't like he had to go to the east side for them.

The head of personnel of this firm also sees transportation as a problem for city workers, but noted that it was

not a major problem . . . we have employees that will call in and say my car broke down, but is it transportation problems that's getting them fired? Usually no. We've only probably had to fire 4 people, ever, and 2 were due to attendance and they were both alcoholic problems.

On the other hand, two interviewed employers do not believe their workers when they say they have transportation problems. The first is the floor supervisor at Curve-All, who says that most of his workforce relies on the bus, which he states is a

big problem. . . . Lots of times what they do, they'll call and say, well I'm going to be late because my bus didn't come. And a lot of times it'll be like 5 minutes till seven, and they just woke up, and I already know that, so. It goes, it's like a game, I know. Sometimes you get maybe, I'll watch, and sometimes you might get like 4 people come in at one time, and they'll be off the seven o'clock that I know is pretty much the bus. But you'll get like one come in, say like a couple of people ride the same bus, one comes in at 6:50 and one comes in at 7:15, and another comes in at 7:35, and say, oh, my bus didn't come on time.

The white floor supervisor at Sears Metals similarly states: "Well, I had one guy who told me that in order to get here by six o'clock, he had to get on the bus at 4:30, and he only lived like 10 miles from here. That doesn't make a whole lot of sense to me. I mean, he could have walked in faster than that," a statement which may just point to this respondent's lack of knowledge about the inefficiencies in Detroit's bus system.

In contrast, a white MCSUI respondent who managed a downtown Detroit retail establishment summed up the problems of public transportation and low-wage work in a very articulate way:

most of my girls take a bus . . . transportation is poor. Well that doesn't
help people moving around a city who are trapped in a city or can't get
out of the city or have the mobility to go and get a better job or even
move around to find a better job. The hours of the transportation
system are terrible, the girls have to wait. You talk about a woman
going out on the street standing at a bus stop. One of my girls came in
the other day and the woman standing next to her had her purse
snatched.

He further notes that "the bus costs $1.50 per day, and a transfer is
$.50," and he says it would take several transfers to make it to a job in
Southfield, the integrated northwestern suburb where the respondent
lives.

SUBURBAN EMPLOYERS, TRANSPORTATION, AND DISCRIMINATORY HIRING PRACTICES

All of the four suburban white-owned firms interviewed as part of this
study cited transportation problems as the reason for having few (or no)
African-American workers. For example, the manager of USG, a
propane company in the suburb of Trenton (which is located about 10
miles south of the city of Detroit), stated that only one person out of his
workforce of 10 is black because: "Well, I think the surrounding area,
you know, the people that we're drawing from, just for whatever reason
haven't applied here or they don't want to travel out this far." However,
they do have a few white workers from Detroit, and three white workers
who live in a rural area that is "45 minutes away from here . . . 8 miles
north of the Ohio border."

Mash Inc. is in Roseville, located a few miles north of the city of Detroit. The firm's CEO gave the following as a reason for that fact that his
workforce is only 3 percent black:

> . . . I think in part because we are as far north as we are, and because of
> transportation, basically transportation issues, we tend not to get a
> great deal of black applicants. . . . There's no public transportation. We
> had one kid, who's no longer with us, but he used to take like two buses
> and walk like two miles to get to work every day. It was incredible, it
> was just incredible.

Similarly, the CEO of Mushroom Plastics, which is located in War-

ren adjacent to the northern border of Detroit, explains the fact that his
workforce is only 5 percent African American by stating that although all
of his workforce is drawn from a "10-mile radius," blacks have no transportation to his plant (Detroit is just over one mile away.) He was not
sure if any of his workers lived in the city of Detroit:

> I don't know the answer to that. . . . There's no public transportation
> system for them to get up here. We do monitor our minorities, but I'm
> not sure, we don't monitor where they live, I don't think. We have peo-
> ple in Detroit, we're on the borderline, I can't tell you that. We're pretty
> close to Eight Mile Road, so my guess is, sure.

The head of personnel for Mushroom also blames transportation for
the low number of African Americans among their workers: "We're not
on a bus line so, yeah, you'd have to have a car." She also had more information about where workers live:

> . . . we draw mainly from this area, but we do have people from, we
> don't really have very many people that live in Oakland County but we
> have people from Detroit and then we have some that live way out.
> There's quite a few actually that live around Port Huron area, Romeo,
> out in the country, quite far away [these locations are about 20 miles
> away].

This respondent later stated that she had formerly been in personnel
for the hotel and restaurant industry in the suburbs of Detroit where
nearly all the housekeeping staff was black. When asked how much of
the low percentage of blacks in suburban auto-supply plants was a function of poor transportation options, or just habits of the industry, she
replied: "I think it's more habits in the industry, for some reason. Most of
the housekeeping staff were all black, at least in the experiences I've had,
for some reason."

Finally, the CEO of Janis Snap and Tool (which has a 100 percent
white workforce) states that they draw from Clinton Township, Mount
Clemens, Roseville, and East Pointe, all northeastern suburbs, "so everybody's pretty local." The plant manager for this firm notes that they don't
hire anyone from Detroit, because:

> . . . maybe because we don't advertise. We get the occasional guy that
> is literally on a job hunt so he's dropping applications every which way

but loose. And you don't generally run into people from Detroit. They're generally from this local area.

This respondent brings a key explanation for low minority representation in suburban firms into the discussion: hiring and recruitment methods. The hiring and recruitment strategies of black and white case-matched suburban firms are compared in the next section of this chapter, which concludes with 3 case studies (culled from MCSUI interviews) of successfully integrated white-owned suburban firms, and suggests that the key component in their success are strongly enforced affirmative action guidelines.

A COMPARISON OF HIRING AND RECRUITMENT METHODS OF SIX CASE-MATCHED SUBURBAN FIRMS

Mash Inc. and Twain Industries

Mash Inc. is a manufacturer of small stamped metal and plastic parts. This is a highly automated facility: according to the CEO, jobs either require high skills or fairly low skills. Automation has resulted in the firm having more highly skilled workers than machine operators (the sample job). Machine operators generally check the operation of automated stamping machines and check parts for faults. Only 7 out of 76 operators are African American. Wages are $7.15 to start, but workers are raised to $9.00/hour within a year. The CEO of Mash reported that machine operators can make up to $25,000/year with overtime.

This firm recruits operators solely by putting a sign in the window. To explain the rationale for this, the CEO stated:

> Well, again, people know Groesbeck Highway. I'm going to go look for a job. What are you going to do? I'm going to get in the car and I'm going to start at Eight Mile, and I'm going to drive. And anyplace there's a sign, I'm going to go in, and maybe if the sign's not out, I'm going to go in and say are you taking applications.

This statement assumes that applicants have cars and that they are not subject to police scrutiny if they continually stop in the Groesbeck Corridor. Yet this firm has still managed to hire and retain a workforce that is 9 percent black.

Mash's match, the minority-owned and operated Twain Plastic

Products, is located in Troy, Michigan, which is about 5 miles northwest of Roseville and 8 miles from the city line. This firm starts workers at $5.71/hour, or 35 percent less than Mash Inc. Average wages differ by 38 percent ($6.33 versus $10.20). The sample job at Twain is also a machine operator—beginning workers pull parts off the molding machine, trim them, and check them for faults. Eighty-eight percent of the 45 operators employed at Twain are African American.

Twain primarily uses Detroit newspapers to hire. However, the CEO has recently decided to advertise in the suburban Macomb Daily because he would like to attract what he feels are higher-skilled white suburban workers. According to this respondent, the newspaper in which an employer places an ad determines the skill level as well as the race of the applicant. When he places an ad in the Detroit papers, he reports that 90 percent of the applicants are black:

> . . . because again, we were advertising in the Detroit News and there are some clear signals in this area. When you want to hire black general laborers, everybody in the industry knows you put it in the Detroit News. That's the signal to the whole world. If you're not interested in hiring black employees, you put it in the Macomb Daily.

Twain's CEO does not believe in using informal methods, such as word of mouth, to recruit workers, since workers who know each other may not at all have similar work habits. He also does not perform either drug or criminal screens when hiring because:

> . . . we know that a large portion of this group is going to be eliminated. Drugs are an illness in our society and if a minority company is going to tell you two things, no drugs and no police record, we've eliminated 90 percent of the black applicants, especially the black males. So we're worried about this day forth, but we don't allow any drugs on you or in you, alcohol on you or in you, and you're not allowed to smoke in our facilities. We're not tolerant at all.

The young African-American supervisor at Twain reported that fully 70 percent of the machine operators do not have cars; nearly all arrive from Detroit and "get dropped off or they ride with someone." Workers arrange carpools, and some take the bus. If workers live in Detroit, they must take at least two buses to get to work: the CEO notes that workers can take a Detroit bus to the Oakland shopping mall, and then take another bus to their plant, which is a mile away.

It is interesting that Twain Plastics manages to attract a carless, majority-black workforce to Troy to take jobs that pay very low wages. For every ad the CEO places in the Detroit papers, he notes that he receives over three hundred applications, mostly from black Detroiters. He believes that he is clearly an exceptional suburban employer. He believes that black economic gains are eroding because of

> clearer levels of discrimination. The society is far more discriminatory today than it has ever been in my lifetime. I mean, it's just the fact that the discrimination that I mentioned to you this morning, the subtle things that you notice in the papers, there's just certain areas where blacks find it very difficult to be employed. Troy is one of them. I guarantee you, probably half of the black employees in the whole Troy area probably work right here.

Mushroom Plastics and Elizabeth Plastic Products

Mushroom Plastics is a family-run business that is located in Warren. The workforce is described as being less than 5 percent black. The firm's CEO was hesitant to tell me the wages paid to his predominantly female workforce, but did say that he started workers with the "community wage" of $8-9/hour. The sample job at Mushroom is a machine operator, which the CEO considers to be "light work." This is the suburban employer mentioned earlier who said he employed so few blacks because he only drew from a "10-mile radius" which he said includes "only the real north end of the city." Since he is located at 9 1/2 Mile Road in Warren (miles are measured from downtown Detroit), a 10-mile radius actually includes the entire city of Detroit.

The CEO at Mushroom stated they hire exclusively through word of mouth. This might have been true once, but the director of personnel later reported they hire exclusively through temporary agencies. She uses 5 different agencies, and all are located in the northern suburbs. All of the agencies send only white workers to this organization; the personnel director stated that the few black workers that are now at the plant date from the time before they started using temps. She additionally noted that she usually goes "through 20 [temps] before I make a decision on hiring one person" and that about 85 percent of these workers desire permanent employment, facts that point to an indication of a surplus of white workers seeking entry-level jobs in the suburbs.[5]

Mushroom's case match, Elizabeth Products, is located in Roseville, about 2 miles east of Mushroom Plastics (about the same distance from the city of Detroit as Mushroom). Elizabeth also manufactures plastic parts, using methods similar to Mushroom's. The entry-level workforce here is about 65 percent black, and most workers are women. The sample jobs for both firms are parallel—machine operators. However, the entry-level wage at Elizabeth is $5.45/hour, which is 36 percent less than the approximately $8.50/hour paid at Mushroom.

Elizabeth also uses temporary agencies, although they also hire walk-ins, who are referred by word of mouth. The head of personnel for this firm, who is a black woman, notes that she prefers to hire friends rather than relatives when she uses word of mouth referrals (she does not want to be involved in family problems). The white floor supervisor, who began at Elizabeth when this firm was white-owned and operated, notes that most of the temp workers sent over are black. Neither the head of personnel nor the supervisor noted problems with transportation; the supervisor says the majority of black workers take the bus to work.

Although both the CEO and the personnel director at Mushroom give the fact that they are not on a bus line as the rationale for their relative lack of black workers (they are in fact on several bus lines), African-American workers are able to take buses both to Elizabeth Products and Twain Plastics, which are located even further than Mushroom Products from the city of Detroit.

Janis Snap and Tool and Lionel Plastics

Lionel Plastics is a partially black-owned firm located on Ten Mile Road in Roseville. They primarily use both city and suburban newspapers to recruit workers. The white head of personnel for Lionel notes that 50 percent of the applicants are African American. At this point in time, 35 percent of the entry-level workforce is black. The black floor supervisor says that nearly all of his employees get to work by car; the head of personnel says that some Detroiters rely on public transportation.

Janis Snap and Tool is a family-owned and run business that is located on Twelve Mile Road in Roseville (it is 4 miles from the Detroit border of Eight Mile Road). This firm has 75 employees, and about 5 are in unskilled entry-level positions. In this metal stamping plant people are hired in as maintenance workers and are then promoted into machine-operator positions as they become open. Workers are hired in at $10.00/hour (33 percent more than the starting wage at Lionel of $6.70/hour). Only a few operator positions are described as "women's work" (hand-feed jobs that require dexterity); at the time of the interview all operators were men.[6] This firm is 100 percent white at all levels.

This firm hires exclusively by word of mouth and walk-ins. The CEO reported that they recruit through newspaper advertisements and word of mouth; he also noted that they occasionally use temp agencies. The plant manager reported that the company recruits solely through word of mouth and walk-ins:

> We do not actively recruit even as far as want ads. You can easily be accused of prejudice for not . . . by not just actively taking strictly walk-ins you can be accused of that. We found that out about 6 months ago. We weren't accused of anything, but one of our attorneys . . . sent us a letter and current law situation and how it was being interpreted, but if you were strictly hiring by word of mouth that was considered prejudiced hiring practices.

This plant manager formerly worked at a partially black-owned foundry located in New Haven, a suburban city about 20 miles north of Detroit, which employs a large number of African Americans. This respondent once supervised a primarily black workforce and seemed surprised about the racial composition he sees in suburban Detroit plants. When asked if there were any black workers at Janis even during the probation period, he replied:

> No. Yeah, I don't know whether it's coincidental, as much as I guess if you look at it honestly you would say that it is not that. . . . And one that obviously if someone questioned it, you know it was wrong, but I think it's also one that people have adapted in this area that says, "Okay, as long as we don't actively recruit in that area, then we don't have to deal with it." And I'm amazed when I went from the area that I left, into this environment, that it even existed. I couldn't even believe that it existed.

He further noted that the situation of recruiting and hiring a totally white workforce was occurring: "Because they can get away with it here . . . 'cause no one's ever called them on it." He then, with historical accuracy, described why they "couldn't get away with it" in the foundry he formerly worked in:

> There, if you went back 30 years ago, when the workforce became es-
> tablished up there, they hired many, many people from the South. They
> actually went down and actively recruited because they couldn't get
> workers. There was a boom time here, and they couldn't pull people
> into their foundry and then they started a lot of black people there by
> choice, and it just kind of continued from there. Then it was basically
> anybody. In a place that's that isolated, I think that you get many more
> applications from people .... If they're coming from Port Huron
> they're going to stop at a place that employs 1,000 people, and they're
> going to put in an application, rather than come into a place that em-
> ploys 75 people. There's not the same kind of traffic, as far as applica-
> tions go.

He concludes:

> But again it really is. . . . It's a situation where I think that people fear
> that once they have the first black person, female, you know. . . . Right
> or wrong, I think that they're saying, "Okay, now we're dealing with a
> different set of rules." I think it's kind of got to mirror a much bigger
> picture than just this industry. It's real, I mean for us to say that it's not
> real. I don't know that I could have a straighter conversation with any-
> body else, but I mean, it's real. . . . There's a true prejudice and it does
> exist in this world, and if anybody else says it doesn't, just doesn't pay
> any attention.

These white suburban employers do not use Detroit newspapers or agencies and organizations that handle black as well as white applicants; instead, they use informal recruitment mechanisms (such as word of mouth, or a sign in the window), which tend to result in the replication of the characteristics of their existing (white) workforces.

How prevalent are these practices? It is very difficult to get a sense of this without resorting to an audit methodology to test hiring discrimi-nation. However, Federal Employment Commission auditors found an 18.9 percent rate of discrimination in the District of Columbia and a 37.2 percent rate in its two surrounding suburban areas.[7]

In addition, the cases of the suburban black-owned companies that have managed to employ relatively large numbers of blacks at firms that are located at least as far from the residences of urban African Americans as white-owned firms provide a contrast to white-owned firms that use hiring and recruitment practices that have the effect of discouraging the applications of black workers.

MCSUI CASE STUDIES

Like the black employers profiled above, there appears to be evidence among the employers I interviewed as part of the Detroit Multi-City Survey of Urban Inequality (MCSUI) that those who are legally required to hire minority workers manage to employ comparatively large percentages of African-American workers in firms that are located some distance away from central-city black populations.

Noted here are 3 large firms: 2 are corporations with national and international markets, the 3rd is a public utility.[8] In one organization, a Big Three auto manufacturer, antidiscrimination measures were imposed and enforced through governmental contract requirements as well as UAW efforts; the utility based its affirmative action program on local and federal mandates for public sector employers, and the third firm, a large national retailer, implemented strong antidiscrimination measures through court order: in 1984 they lost a federal lawsuit brought forth by workers alleging racial and gender discrimination.

A BIG THREE AUTO MANUFACTURING FACILITY

The Firm in Its Setting: Warren

This plant is located in Warren, which, as described earlier, is a predominantly white, Polish-American, blue-collar suburb of Detroit located just north of the eastern part of the city across Eight Mile Road. Warren has a reputation for racism on the part of employers, residents, and police. Warren is also the home of many smaller auto-supply companies in the Detroit metropolitan area which, based on this and the MCSUI study, had very few African-American workers.

This plant has been in Warren for many years, and is adding workers at the present time. They had not done any hiring for years up until August 1993, when they added one thousand people. Over ten thousand people are employed at this complex, and four thousand work in the facility where I held my interviews. Over eight hundred workers are employed in the "sample job"—unskilled assembler. Of these, 18 percent are women and 56 percent are African American (there are also a few Latinos, and a large population of Arab Americans, who are not considered to be minority workers). The workforce of the supervisor I interviewed is 65 percent black. Thirty-five percent of the department are women and 60 percent of the women are African American.

The director of personnel said the plant was 56 percent black because "we are as close to Detroit as you can get." He stated that this percentage is much higher than that at other Warren firms because:

> . . . we would be more attuned [to discrimination issues] because of the size of the corporation, we would be more in tuned to the various federal and state [laws]. We are more susceptible . . . and more sensitive . . . we look at the demographics and the ability of the workforce around the location, what lives in the city, what's close by. We have a responsibility to the citizens of the city to hire the people that live here.

Black and White Workers Compared

The personnel director also stated that he did not see skill or turnover differences between white and black workers. He attributed this to the fact that he has an older workforce: "I mean you don't do stupid things at 40 that you did at 20. The older workers as a group have similar skills, that on the whole are not as good as those of the newer workers." The personnel director stated that it is too early to tell whether there are racially determined skill differences among the newer workers. He noted some racial differences in communication skills, but stated they did not hamper work:

> I don't see that [black English] as a problem and I don't see that as something my customers should be concerned about. I think my customer is number one. I want to give my customer the best quality product I can for his dollar, and whether I have an Arab that speaks Arabic with broken English, if I have black man who speaks black English, if I have a Polish guy who can't talk, if I have a white guy who is the best speaker in the world, or all women, black or white, I don't care. Their focus and their attention is to provide the customer with the best quality product they can produce. I don't see where their speech patterns or tendency would have any effect on it.

Relationships Between Black and White Employees

This firm's personnel director also stated that he does not have any problems with blacks and whites getting along on the floor:

> . . . a lot of them recognize the fact that they probably spend more time here than they do at home with their families and this almost becomes like a family to them, either within their work cell, or their work group, or their work department, and there is an inner relationship that doesn't focus on who you are, what color you are, where you are from. . . . I think there is a tendency: "don't even pay attention." It's like you're on the job and say, "hey, Suzy, what the hell did you do last night?" "Oh, the old man got mad because I didn't press his shorts or something." I think there is more interaction on what you did at home, how you feel, did you go out and get stupid last night, Tigers lost another one, Lions stink . . . whereas I think I'm black, you're white, he's Arab, we don't get along. I don't see that from my perspective at all.

On the other hand, the floor supervisor noted racial differences in work ethic and attitude, but only until black workers feel they "are part of the team." He states that other employers may say there are differences between whites and blacks

> because they were raised in the '60s and '70s . . . I come from a Polish family and my brother is definitely . . . hates blacks with a passion. He works for the city of Detroit, and he has them tagged as lazy, no good, SOBs. I have worked with a number of blacks that I probably wouldn't trade for friends that I have known for years, because they are basically good people. Sure, they're black. Who cares?

The supervisor saw no differences in skills between either black or whites, or city and suburban workers. He noted that:

> . . . it's all in the perception of the person . . . [that he hears] "oh, he's black, he's no good." That's bull. I have for years, I have always contended there are people I don't like whether they are black or white. I wouldn't even want them living next door to me. It's the same way out here. My business is to build vehicles and that is what I tell my people. We are here to do one thing only, build that vehicle and make money. To make money it don't matter if we are black, white, green, or purple.

All we are concerned with is building that truck. As long as that is built with quality and the job is done right, we have no problem.

The supervisor states he has a majority black workforce because the major hiring for his department was done in the 1960s and '70s (when antidiscrimination measures were implemented). He said that there was still quite a lot of in-migration of both black and white southerners during this time and that people "poured into the Warren plant" and it "became a boiling pot of closed plants in the Detroit area." He also mentions that they hired a lot of inner-city black workers during those years.

Wages, Skills, and Worker Attitudes

Like many supervisors of comparatively high-wage entry-level jobs, this floor supervisor tended to blame the low wages that are offered for most entry-level jobs on the employment problems of Detroit workers, rather than on the workers themselves:

> I think wage dictates a lot, although all the economists say that wages don't mean nothing. When you look at a vehicle, I happen to work in the car industry, let's look at a car or a home. A young person coming out of, let's say, high school, going into a $6/hour job, is not going to afford a $15,000-$30,000 car. He can't get married unless he marries someone that is also working and between the two of them they are making $12/hour, and even that is pushing the line. . . . I think wages or the economy has outgrown what wage scales should be at. Face it, could you live on $4/hour or whatever the hell is that minimum wage is: $4.25/hour? Could you as a young person coming out of high school or out of college, maybe college is a bad example to use, but I see a lot of them out there trying to scuffle to make $5/hour right now. Realistically, live on your own as an independent person without going out begging for help, you can't do it.

He continues:

> I make good money, I'll be the first to admit it. I've worked for (this firm) going on 30 years in September. . . . I have my bitches about certain things, but I have a good wage, I've raised a family, I have a nice home, I buy myself a new car every 3 or 4 years. My wife has a car, my wife is not working . . . basically, we live on my wage, but I make good money. At least when you are making 17-20 bucks an hour, you can do

things. Maybe we can't afford a $150,000 house, but you can afford a $50,000-70,000 home. You can afford a roof over your head.

When asked why there are not more black workers in Warren, he replied:

[It's] something about hiring policies. . . . I know Warren has been up for several lawsuits for not hiring blacks versus whites . . . in some cases it's true, and in some [it's not]. As far as discrimination goes, I think the majority of it is the same, and I think it's always going to be there. It's a black and white thing and that's it.

A PUBLIC UTILITY: DETROIT GAS

The Firm in its Setting: Royal Oak

Royal Oak is a mostly white, solidly middle-class city located northwest of Detroit. A core of well-kept-up older homes is surrounded by newer homes; there has recently been construction in this area. There is a small downtown that has been gentrified in recent years: it is home to a vital live theater and many offbeat and expensive shops.

This public utility is a regional headquarters that supplies power for Wayne, Oakland, and Macomb counties. There are 4 other major offices—in Livonia, Pontiac, Macomb County, and Royal Oak—where people report to do service work. The sample job that we built the interview around is that of a customer service representative (complaint and information clerk). This is where the majority of their new hires work when they come into this organization.

A 25 Percent Minority Workforce

Of the 96 clerks in this department, 90 percent are women and 24 percent are African American. The main contact person quoted here is the head of personnel; the supervisor of the consumer service representatives was also interviewed. The personnel director reported that consumer reps are about 25 percent minority because:

. . . all of our hiring is based on mirrored goals and utilization reports that are developed between the company and EEOC. We have certain targets that we are expected and want to meet; we want to mirror the community that we live in and the Detroit area is a very diverse community, and we feel we should be just as diverse as a company.

The racial profile has changed over the past 10 years, and gender changes (with more women as service people) have occurred within the past 5 years. The personnel director reported that minority distribution in meter-reading jobs is the same as it is in clerk jobs.

Racial Relations Among Workers

The personnel director emphasized that with the "sophisticated" workforce that he draws from (compared to that in his last job in a rural community in Ohio), he has "much less problem with minority concerns, or with people working with minorities" than in Ohio (which had a 10-15 percent minority workforce). He said there was no overt tension in Ohio, but much more

> old school mentality—white males in particular, in their attitude or their approach to working with women or minorities. . . . I think people in Detroit . . . I don't know what they really think. I hear a lot up here about how Detroit is so polarized and this and that. I don't know what they really think but they know enough here to know, and say, and for the most part, do the right thing. . . . I mean there's [racial] tension . . . I mean there's a normal amount of tension. Some tension is a good tension actually, and it means we're kind of pushing the limit with the way people think. We are forcing them to evaluate prejudices and I don't think tension is bad necessarily. But I don't see a tension I am really concerned about in this location. We have in our company a group of minority and women management team that meets with my level, my manager, and myself. We meet on a quarterly basis [to address recruiting, training, and education issues].

Recruitment and Minority Worker Representation

Most of this utility's applicants come from Oakland and Wayne Counties, and from the city of Detroit (the latter, about 25 percent). Very few come from the immediate area (defined as a 3-mile radius). Although most people drive 15-20 minutes to work, they have a few people coming from as far away as Flint (25 miles north). The personnel director noted that most of the minority workforce commutes 5 or more miles from Detroit. He mentioned that on a recent open-application day, most of the thousand people who showed up were from Detroit: "[W]e don't have any problems with them getting here."

He said they don't have any problems either recruiting or retaining minority employees because most workers see this utility "as a desirable place to work in the community because it seems to be a stable company . . . so a lot of people don't leave once they get here." (Wages are also comparatively very high: the average wage for a customer service representative is $17/hour; benefits are also very generous.)

When asked why this utility is able to keep such a high percentage of minority workers in the face of extensive organizational and technical change, the personnel director replied:

> our ability to recruit appropriately, with the test it really helps. We get a higher caliber, it doesn't matter, male, female, minority, it doesn't matter. We get a higher caliber, but certainly that minority candidate coming in has to meet that minimum requirement, which is a pretty high requirement.

They recruit through "open application days"; as noted, over one thousand people showed up at the last one. They also have about "10 or 15 referral agencies"—MESC and minority organizations—but they are often unhappy with applicants referred by them. New workers are watched carefully, their calls are monitored sporadically, and they have review sessions every week.

However, the personnel director says he "definitely" sees geographic differences in applicants' ability to pass their entrance test. He guess that about 20 percent more suburban applicants' pass the test than city applicants. They have very few white people from the city who apply, and virtually no black suburbanites, so this difference can be seen as racial as well. Applicants are tested for basic math and reading comprehension skills. He responded to the notion that blacks do not have adequate communications skills with the statement: "that's ridiculous, because half the customer base they deal with is minority." He stated he does not have difficulty finding black workers with good communication skills.

Maintaining an Integrated Workforce

In spite of black reps' poorer showing as group on the employee entrance test, the personnel director notes that the number of black reps in the organization is still higher than what they are required to have, and he attributes this to word of mouth referrals from existing workers: "They know our work, they know what we expect, and we get a lot of people that way." He also mentioned that over 50 percent of supervisors in this utility are minority, and he didn't think one of them lives in Detroit (he didn't know if they were raised outside of the city or moved out once they got better jobs. He said this in the context of discussing the importance of environment in the success of Detroit's young people. He concluded the interview by saying:

> . . . we do go through turnover more with minorities, but we continue to do it . . . but it's difficult for me sometimes when I have to go . . . hiring a line manager who actually does the hiring, and I'm the HR guy, and I've got to somehow convince him to give another chance because he's tired and the supervisors are tired of all the extra work, because it's a lot more work to get rid of a problem employee than it does obviously, to get one who's motivated. You have to deal with all that stuff. I mean it does take a certain commitment on the part of the organization . . . today we're just going to do it . . . we know it's going to take more time and it's going to be more effort, maybe, and you bear it out.

A MAJOR NATIONAL RETAILER: HAMMERS AND CROCKETT DEPARTMENT STORE

The Firms in Their Settings: Waterford and Livonia

Two Hammers and Crockett department stores were randomly selected for face-to-face interviews from the MCSUI base of five hundred firms. One of the stores is located in Waterford, a predominantly white, blue-collar/middle-class suburb in northern Oakland County located just outside the city of Pontiac ("city" workers, this case, refer to residents of Pontiac). The second store is located in Livonia, a white, middle-class to upper-middle-class suburb located west of the city of Detroit.

In 1984, women and minority workers launched a federal lawsuit against this corporation; they alleged both racial and gender discrimination. They won a large settlement, and in addition, the court ordered the implementation of strong antidiscrimination measures. I learned of this lawsuit after completing these interviews.

Hammers and Crockett: Waterford

Workforce Composition. The respondents at the Waterford store were the director of personnel and the sales manager in home improvement. At this location, 225 out of 300 total employees were sales workers. Fifty percent of these workers were white, 42 percent were black, and the remainder were Hispanic (5 percent) or Asian American. Sixty percent of salespeople were women, while 50 percent of the African-American sales workers were female. Fifty-five percent of all sales workers were in commission sales (many selling "big-ticket" items, such as appliances), while about 50 percent of black salespeople received commissions.

Employer Perceptions and Attitudes about Skill Differences Among Workers. Both respondents saw strong locational differences in the skills of workers. The sales manager noted that blacks and whites from Pontiac resemble each other in terms of skills they bring to the job, and that suburban black workers more closely resemble suburban whites than city blacks. He also did not think that skill levels have deteriorated among black workers, and felt that differences among workers are not racially determined but are "an economic thing, where they grow up and how they were raised."

The sales manager also stated that he feels that both black and white kids from the city of Pontiac "are tougher kids who have experienced more hard times." Although he thought that they tended to have more trouble with the job, he tried to give them a chance. He also stated that you can see in the application that Pontiac kids are less educated than suburban kids. It is he who noted that "the spelling is terrible and the English is terrible," however, he feels they can communicate verbally much better than they can on paper.

The personnel director reported that work ethic and attitude among workers have worsened in recent years; especially among young people, and that parents are the cause. However, she does not see any gender or racial differences in this trend. She feels that rural people are more dependable than urban or suburban residents, and that urban residents are the least dependable. This is so, she says, because they have more opportunity to "jump from one place to another."

When asked why she thought that blacks may be doing more poorly in the labor market, the personnel director responded that it may be their attitudes: "Well, there are only a few that might have a little grudge on their shoulder that they haven't had enough in their life, not a lot."

A Worker Shortage in Waterford. Both respondents complained that they have a lot of problems attracting workers to Hammers and Crockett. The sales manager stated that this problem is due to the wage offered: "[I]t's not economical to accept these jobs" (salespeople start at $5.02/hour). The personnel director stated that she has a difficult time attracting workers because of increasing retail competition. Retail has "bloomed" in area in last 15 years, and now stores are "all fighting one another."

Because of the store's location, the personnel director reported that she could employ people who live in the city, in suburban, and rural areas—she attracts people from as far away as Flint. She notes that some Detroit residents try to work there, but "they never stay" because of travel time (45 minutes to one hour).

Both respondents report that they do not get enough people through word of mouth and walk-ins. Openings are advertised in the Oakland Press (a suburban paper) as well as in tricounty employment guides. The personnel director also calls schools and colleges as well as some retirement areas.

Hammers and Crockett: Livonia

The Livonia contacts are the director of personnel and an assistant sales manager in the lawn and garden shop. The Livonia branch of Hammers and Crockett is the largest in the country. Once there were 1,500 employees at this location, but automation and recent financial constraints have reduced this number to about 450 workers. There are about 100 full-time workers; the rest are part-time workers.

Workforce Composition. Forty percent of the Livonia sales force is black; the personnel director seemed to waffle when asked how many blacks were in commission sales. The sales manager stated that less than half of the black workers work on commission; among all workers, she noted that maybe "about 75 percent" are in commission sales.

At Livonia, 90 percent of salaried (noncommission) sales workers are women. Sixty percent of commission sales workers are men. Commission salespeople "make quite a bit of money," as much as $60,000/year in this location, as so much of their commission sales are big-ticket items.

Customer Discrimination. The head of personnel reported that she has received letters from white customers stating that they will not shop at the Livonia store because black people are selling to them. She does not think this is common, however. She said: "[blacks] are as equal as we are, until, I mean and for promotions and anything like that. I think that if they are as good as this white person, then boy, both of them should be considered as equals, and I think it's wrong to . . . [discriminate]. I just hope that when I leave everybody else feels the same way too."

Perceptions of Worker Skill Differences. She reported that the communication skills of black workers have improved in the recent year:

> Did you see me come out? When I came out to meet you there was a black gal there that had some papers in her hand and I looked right at her and said "Susan?" I knew . . . I assumed you were white, really I did, from your telephone conversation, but I think it's the greatest thing in the world when I don't know.

In spite of the fact that she reported that communication skills are improving among African Americans, she still believed there are differences between blacks and whites, and that "black English" is a major reason for prejudice against workers: "I don't think they should do that. I think that is a number one prejudice that can be eliminated." She also believed that employers are turned off by black English: "I don't want to know when I pick up the phone whether you are black or white."

This personnel director saw no racial differences in applications ("some are a mess, some are terrific . . . I certainly look twice at a good application"). She did see big differences in the skill levels of those who went to Detroit schools and those who attended suburban schools, except for those from Cass Tech, a magnet school that requires an entrance exam in Detroit. She said "they are the cream of the crop," and are equal to those who went to Livonia schools.

The sales manager also saw differences in communication skills between black and white workers. When asked, she said that this probably doesn't affect sales, but "it might hurt the productivity of the department as a whole in general depending on what ratio you have, and if it's a problem or not a problem. If you have someone that's a minority and communication isn't there and they're not developing as a sales associate, I think that would cause a problem." She noted that this is an infrequent problem, and that it is also a problem of white associates as well.

This manager notes clear class differences between white and black workers, saying that blacks often come from poorer background than the middle-class white workers. She feels that about half the black workers at Hammers and Crockett are middle class. Lawson feels that skill differences seem to arise more out of the backgrounds that people have rather than their race. When discussing a woman with poor communication skills, she said "in the instance that I am thinking about, she was white, and did not have very much money as far as dressing properly for work and what have you . . . so I think that it might have more of a background that you come from rather than race."

Yet she states that it would be more difficult to find a black salesperson with the abilities to sell tractors than it would be for her to find black workers to sell lingerie. When asked why, she said, "[E]ducation and experience. Most of the people that work for me have had experience. You don't come across many black applicants who have had experience at selling big-ticket commission items." They do not require that commission sales workers have previous experience in commission sales.

The sales manager felt that black women are as likely to have sales experience as white women; their experience tends to be at fast-food outlets, and their tenure at previous jobs is shorter on average than that of white women (who often had experience in retail stores as well as in fast food).

Recruitment. The personnel director reported that they have more minorities applying, whereas they once had to recruit from Detroit high schools to get minority candidates. She attributed this to bus transportation (there was none 10-15 years ago).[9] She noted that most black workers come by bus from Detroit. She was not aware of any white workers from the city. She thought that word of mouth is responsible for the number of black workers they have (she noted that few area stores employ many black workers):

> One guy that works here lives in downtown Detroit near the Renaissance Center [a distance over 20 miles away] . . . and takes two buses or something to get here every day. And word might get out. You do get people that come in and fill out applications that know someone who works here, has a relative that works here . . . word might get out that Hammer does hire here.

SOME OBSERVATIONS ABOUT MANDATED SUBURBAN INTEGRATION

Varying Employer Attitudes

All three of these firms may be viewed as success stories when it comes to the sheer numbers of minority workers present compared to racial distributions in similar firms in these locations. However, employer perceptions and attitudes vary within these firms. The employers who saw the greatest differences between blacks and whites, and were least likely to perceive either class or geographic differences as explanations for racial skill disparities, were associated with Hammers and Crockett and Detroit Gas, both which are located the farthest away from the city of Detroit of the companies interviewed and have the shortest histories of worker integration; Hammers was also forced to integrate under duress.

On the other hand, the personnel director of Detroit Gas is a white employer in a majority-white suburb who appeared to be unenthusiastic about the idea of mandated affirmative action goals, but also seemed honestly to be trying to grapple with the implications of such mandates. Although he noted clear differences in the abilities of white and black workers either to pass the entrance exam or retain their jobs once they were hired, he stressed that he was able to maintain minority worker representation so that it consistently exceeded required levels.

The attitudes of the respondents at the Big Three auto plants seemed different than those of the others described in this chapter section. Perhaps their more positive comments reflect the fact that they, among all the employers at the three cases, had the most number of years to adjust to both the reality and idea of enforced antidiscrimination measures (each person interviewed had been with the firm for more than 25 years; these policies had been in effect for nearly all of this time).

These respondents also made it clear that they were very committed to their union and its stance on affirmative action, even though they were quick to admit that they themselves did not come from racially tolerant backgrounds.

Affirmative Action and the Persistence of Occupational Segregation

It also appears from these case studies that federal or judicial mandates to hire black workers did not appear adequately to address the issue of persistent occupational segregation. Both Hammers and Crockett department stores are located in malls. The ratio of white to African-American sales workers at Hammers and Crockett appeared to be strikingly different than that of the other outlets, whose racial composition appeared to be nearly exclusively white.

However, although Hammers and Crockett employs a large percentage of black salespeople, their distribution into the higher-paying positions does not reflect their representation on the total workforce. In Livonia, the women's department, where no salesperson works on commission, was 80 percent black (there is only one black worker out of 20 commissioned sales workers in lawn and garden). The sales manager attributes this to the fact that turnover is very low in lawn and garden— these are full-time workers. She also notes that there "are not very many commissioned sales people that are black in this store," although she could not articulate a good reason for this discrepancy.

The discrepancy in occupations (and wages) between the white and black workers in these firms echoes the findings among the case-matched auto-supply firms that black ownership and/or enforced antidiscrimination measures may increase employment, but do not address persistent wage gaps between blacks and whites.

CONCLUSION: RACE AND SPACE

As suggested in the introduction of this chapter, spatial mismatch, often described as one "explaining" variable of worsening wage and employment gaps between blacks and whites, is also an encapsulation of the larger social, economic, and political forces that contribute to inequality and are expressed spatially. Therefore, the existence of a spatial mismatch between urban residents and largely suburbanized jobs and job networks, now unequivocally supported in the literature, begs no simple solution, but a multifaceted ameliorative approach. Such an approach, to be effective, should include increased transportation options between city and suburb, increased affordable housing in the suburbs, and increased measures to combat housing discrimination, as well as incentives for the retention of in-city firms (as long as they pledge to hire local workers). However, in addition to these mechanisms to redress the effects of spatial mismatch, these findings point to the need for antidiscriminatory measures in suburban businesses to ensure the maximization of work opportunities and choices of urban blacks.

It is clear from these findings and from the results of other research studies that spatial mismatch contributes to black-white employment and earnings gaps through the mechanisms of increased information, search, and travel costs that hinder the ability of African Americans to learn about and/or keep jobs located far from them. However, it also appears that spatial mismatch is the result of—and, in a feedback way, the cause of—persistent discrimination. Racially discriminatory attitudes created the federal housing and highway policies that ensured the stark racial divisions between city and suburbs that we see today in the metropolitan Detroit area. This long-lived race-based spatial division has in turn created conditions that increase racial polarization, such as the assurance that segregated blacks have significantly worse schooling and resources than whites because of the flight of residents and capital out of cities. Thus, race, space, and skill issues are necessarily intertwined.

NOTES

[1]For general reviews of the spatial mismatch literature, see Holzer (1991), and Jencks and Mayer (1989).

[2]Because I held interviews at only 6 suburban firms in this study, I will be supplementing this study's findings in regard to space and transportation issues with observations gleaned from suburban respondents that I interviewed as part of the MCSUI effort.

[3]Harassment of blacks in the suburbs was an unexpected finding; there are no questions relating to it in my survey instrument. The fact that this issue was brought up by four individuals without prompting leads me to believe that this phenomenon is more pervasive among respondents than is suggested by what is presented here.

[4]Ford encouraged black workers to live in the neighboring city of Inkster; he financially supported both private businesses and community efforts in the black community there until black workers successfully organized along with whites for the unionization of Ford Motor Company (Turner, 1993).

[5]It has become quite clear to me through my findings that temporary employment agencies, which are being increasingly used in the manufacturing as well as the service sector, are playing a role much like real estate brokers in keeping firms segregated. Blacks are sent to black-owned firms, or firms located in the city of Detroit with many black workers, whites are sent to the suburbs. As part of my MCSUI research I interviewed several personnel managers who represented temporary agencies and were placed on site at plants—one told me that discrimination practiced by most agencies was quite blatant, with employers specifying the race of the workers they sought and the agencies complying. I intend to make this finding the subject of future research.

[6]I did not address gender effects on wage in this study. I did tour all plants where interviews were held, and very few jobs appeared to require any traits that males are more likely to have, such as physical strength (the exceptions were the jobs at the chemical and propane gas companies, as well as the truck and rack repair shops). All necessitated heavy lifting; there seems to be nothing outside of arbitrary gender preference (or wages offered) that appeared to affect the gender composition of machine-operator jobs.

[7]Rates of discrimination were calculated based on two criteria: who in matched pairs proceeded further in the hiring process (i.e., application to phone call to interview to offer), and who received offers.

[8]The fact that these firms are large may contribute to their using antidiscrimination measures. Holzer (1995; 1996) and Kirschenman and Neckerman (1991a) note that small firms are far more likely to rely on informal hiring methods, such as word of mouth, which have a discriminatory effect. Large firms that are government contractors (or the recipients of class-action lawsuits) are also more likely to be scrutinized by regulating agencies.

[9]Improved transportation to this location has pointed to the role of spatial mismatch as another reason this firm once employed fewer blacks.

CHAPTER 6

Race and Skills
The Role of Perceived Skill Differences in the Lower Wages of African-American Workers

This chapter examines whether differences in skill requirements on the part of firms, and/or differences in skill characteristics on the part of workers, may help explain the differences in wages paid by case-matched white- and black-owned firms. When I interviewed employers, I sought to determine whether studied employers perceive racially defined skill differences among workers. I also asked whether they saw skill differences between people who lived in the city and in the suburbs, regardless of race, to see if such "spatially defined" differences may also contribute to a rationale for the wage gaps and differences in the percentage of black employment seen among the case-matched firms.

To provide a context for the findings, I begin with a discussion from the literature about how skill issues are said to contribute to growing wage and employment gaps between young blacks and whites. I then attempt to determine, as some authors suggest in this often equivocal literature, whether studied employers are seeking greater skills from entry-level workers. I also describe what employers who state that they have changed skill demands for studied entry-level jobs mean by "changing skill requirements."

In this sample, representatives from 8 out of 26 surveyed firms stated that they had recently changed their technology or work organization in the past 5 years. Among these firms, 5 reported that they have changed their skill requirements for entry-level workers as a result. The fact that these firms have recently made changes does not necessarily ensure that their skill requirements are greater than those firms that have not recently upgraded—in other words, perhaps some of these firms are merely catching up to where other firms already are. However, their views about work-related changes are presented to present a better sense of how skill-related changes may be affecting the hiring practices of this sample of manufacturers.

An indicator of the relationship between skill demands and wages in this sample may be the comparison of required skills in relatively very high-wage firms and their low-paying matches. Assuming that skill needs and required tasks for the paired firms are matched,[1] if high-paying white owners and poorer-paying black owners have different human-capital needs and differently skilled workers, the wages they pay may reflect these differences.[2] If skill requirements and worker skills, as described by employers,[3] appear to be similar, we can only assume that other factors, such as falling wages among some firms occurring exogenous to skill requirements of the job, local supply and demand characteristics, different production costs and efficiencies, company tradition and history, the payment of efficiency wages, and/or other managerial values may be the reason for the wage differences.

This discussion follows an examination of what white and black respondents have to say about perceived black-white and city-suburban skill differences.

THE PROBLEM AS STATED IN THE LITERATURE: A SKILLS MISMATCH

By 1980, the overall black-white gap in median years of schooling had declined to less than one-half year: 12.6 years for blacks and 13.0 for whites (Jaynes and Williams, 1989). However, as Bound and Freeman found in 1992, the relative earnings of black men fell by 12.1 percent since 1978. They note that the earnings gap between white and black male high school graduates rose from 14.2 percent in 1978 to over 20 percent in 1989. The gap in earnings among black and white college graduates had the biggest jump of all in the 1980s: from 2.5 percent in 1979 to 18.4 percent in 1989. These trends continued through the 1990s (ERP, 1998).

Therefore, as Newman and Stack note, there is a "puzzle" in the research examining growing wage and employment differentials between whites and blacks: "a dramatic convergence in years of education between blacks and whites; coupled with the equally dramatic divergence between racial groups in labor-force participation and wages" (1992). These authors further note "that it would appear that either the quality of education between racial groups differs enough to produce 'human capital' differentials which are in turn reflected in the labor market, or that old fashioned racism is preventing individuals with similar qualifications from finding similar rewards in the marketplace" (p. 11).

One explanation for this seeming contradiction between the growing educational attainment of young African Americans and the relative fall in wages and employment between young blacks and whites rests on the notion that although the absolute education attainment among blacks is increasing relative to whites, it has not kept pace with recent skill demands of jobs (Ferguson, 1995; 1994).

Other authors argue that the quality of black schooling is inferior to that of whites, creating larger "human capital" differentials between the two groups that cannot simply be measured by years of education attained (Orfield, 1992; Newman and Stack, 1992). The human capital explanation, with a focus on "unobservable skill" differences between blacks and whites that cannot be determined simply by educational attainment, has been put forth by O'Neill, who states that demands for skills and abilities *other* than those measured by education shifted in parallel with the demand for educated labor, and that this second shift has set African Americans back in the labor market (1990).

In this vein, Neal and Johnson (1996) found evidence that the black-white wage gap between respondents included in the National Longitudinal Survey of Youth (NLSY) could be nearly completely explained by disparate scores between the two groups on the Armed Forces Qualifying Test (AFQT).

Therefore, if blacks lag behind in skills, increasing demands for skills will put them at an increasing disadvantage. Ferguson argues that the demand for better skills is rising, and therefore there is a premium paid for the types of skills measured by test scores.

However, Moss and Tilly (1991a) note that even if skill demands are rising, evidence linking these shifts to the fate of African Americans is more equivocal. After all, Bound and Freeman found that the deterioration in the black-white wage ratio is not explained by increasing payoffs to education, since the largest deterioration in relative wages is among black college graduates (1992). Holzer is another author who noted that gaps in test scores, as well is in educational levels, between whites and blacks have narrowed in recent years, even while earnings gaps between them have grown (1995).

In addition, Rogers and Spriggs (1996) demonstrated how AFQT scores as predictors of earnings may be racially biased. They note when using components of the test to predict wages of blacks, the effects of verbal scores are significant and positive, while those of math scores are insignificant; these effects are exactly the opposite for whites. Different components of the test are responsible for boosting the wages of each group, which the authors cite as compelling evidence that the score is a racially biased indicator of wages for each group. Additionally, Moss and Tilly (1998) stress that caution should be used in interpreting skill measures that "account" for wage differences: the framework of regression analysis does not establish that differences in test scores cause wage differences, only that differing levels of skills contribute to racial differentials in wage levels.

Another human capital explanation centering on "unobservable" skills has been offered for the eroding economic gains of young African Americans: the notion of a "soft skills" mismatch. Some surveys of employers have found that there are consistent complaints about the attitudes and work behavior of young blacks, particularly young black males (Kirschenman and Neckerman, 1991a, 1991b; Moss and Tilly, 1991b, 1996; Waldinger, 1993).

These increased "soft skill" requirements are not only typical of retail and service jobs where employees have much customer contact, but are also increasingly required in manufacturing jobs, where teamwork and customer contact are newly and increasingly stressed employer requirements (Murnane and Levy, 1994).

Based on the employer interviews they completed in Detroit and Los Angeles, Moss and Tilly have hypothesized that "soft skills," such as motivation and the ability to interact well with customers and co-workers, are becoming increasingly important at a time when many African Americans are said by managers to be especially lacking in such skills (1991b; 1996). These requirements may disproportionately negatively affect young black men, and to a lesser extent, young black women.

William Julius Wilson, in his 1996 book, *When Work Disappears,* placed a strong emphasis on a "soft skills" rationale for why black workers in general—and young black men in particular—are dropping out of the workforce increasing numbers. He noted that 80 percent of interviewed black employers (and 74 percent of whites) who provided comments on job skills, basic skills, work ethic, dependability, attitudes and interpersonal skills expressed negative views of inner-city blacks.

However, there are problems in Wilson's research methodology (most notably that only 57 percent of interviewed employers actually employed black workers), that may have too quickly led him to a notion that inner-city joblessness is far more apt to be the result of "unflattering behaviors" of poor blacks rather than the persistently discriminatory assumptions and hiring practices of employers (see also Turner Meiklejohn, 1999).

Demand-side Skill Changes: Are Skill Needs Increasing?

As noted in chapter 4, many authors have demonstrated that employment has grown in sectors where employees are more highly educated, and shrunk in industries where less-educated workers are more common, and that these shifts have disproportionately hurt African Americans (Moss and Tilly, 1991a; Bound and Freeman, 1992; Carnoy, 1994). Although many researchers have attempted to assess whether skill requirements are actually increasing for low-skilled and semiskilled entry-level jobs, a fact that may also put African Americans at a particular disadvantage, there is little consensus among them.

Osterman (1995), describes skill and training-related findings culled from employer interviews with over seven hundred firms with the statement that "the presumed tendency is now in the direction of upskilling." He also notes that case study findings have been mixed. He cites Flynn (1988) who, in a review of 197 case studies, found empirical support for the stability of skill needs, upskilling, and downskilling.

In his study, Osterman found a trend toward upskilling that was far more pronounced among technical and professional employees than among blue-collar workers, a finding that foreshadows my own recounted here. In addition, blue-collar employers were more likely to define their changing skill needs in terms of behavior (1995). In an earlier study, Mishel and Teixeira suggest that while manufacturing jobs appear increasingly likely to require basic literacy and numeracy, evidence for skill upgrading beyond this level is so far limited to "best practice" companies (1990).

Moss and Tilly have noted that the CEOs and personnel directors they interviewed in Detroit and Los Angeles were likely to say that their skill needs have increased (1991b). Holzer also found that a majority of Detroit and Atlanta-area employers surveyed as part of the MCSUI effort also stated that their skill requirements were increasing for entry-level workers (1995).

However, Fernandez writes that researchers who are attempting to explain racially determined wage and employment gaps have not adequately dealt with the skills mismatch hypothesis; these authors have failed to put

their arguments forth in a contextually grounded concept of skill. Refer-
ring to the work of Moss and Tilly, Fernandez states that they could find no
unequivocal support for the idea that the quality of high school graduates
has declined. Fernandez further notes that most of the existing research relies on workers' education as an exclusive measure of job skills, and that
labor market declines are not only affecting youth—there is a shift away
from black workers of all ages and education levels (1992).

Fernandez favors the work of sociologists Attenwell and Spenner,
who have reviewed a literature that emphasizes the importance of social
and technological context for interpretation of observation and for understanding the nature of skills. Some of this research argues that it is impossible to measure or even conceptualize skill outside of the particular
setting in which work is taking place. Fernandez writes: "[F]or these
scholars the idea of measuring skills mismatch for the economy as a
whole is nonsense" (Fernandez, 1992).

Fernandez also emphasizes that in order actually to gauge whether
there is a mismatch between the skills of workers and the requirements
of jobs, one must directly observe what workers are doing in their jobs,
and how well education is correlated with other skills. This would include the selection of cases where job requirements have changed but job
holders have not, in order to observe these worker's adjustments to
changing job requirements and to determine whether adaptability is correlated with years of education.

Fernandez writes that researchers also need to pay proper attention
to the settings and dimensionality of the concept of skill, including the
inclusion of job analyses, using the *Dictionary of Occupational Titles*
(DOT) as a source. Spenner (1995) notes that the DOT, in their descriptions, integrates two modes of analysis in categorizing jobs. The first addresses the level, scope, and integration of tasks, and the need for mental,
interpersonal, and manipulative skills; the second assesses workers' au-
tonomy and control, including their discretion over content, manner, and
speed with which tasks are done.

Spenner has determined that both of these measures are only mod-
estly related to the educational level of job incumbents (cited in Fernandez, 1992). In addition, Howell and Wolff (1991) have linked the DOT to
census data. They include changing job titles used by the census in an
analysis of whether skill needs are increasing and find what Osterman
calls "mild levels of skill upgrading," although they state that this trend is
expected to level off. Osterman notes that he finds that the DOT-based

studies lack detail; it is impossible to use them to examine changes within occupational titles, which is the focus of this book.

Osterman then critiques a third line of research, which examines trends within a particular industry using surveys in conjunction with DOT-based data (Keefe, 1992). The findings are mixed in these studies as well. The bottom line is that whether technological changes raise, lower, or simply change the level of skills required in new jobs remains an issue that is still debated. As Moss and Tilly note, even if there is strong evidence that skill needs are increasing through time, the central question of relevance here is to what extent changing skill demands have made to the widening of racially determined earnings inequality. They stress that "a simple story of rapid technological change outpacing the skills of inner-city workers of color is too simple a story" (1998, p.15). National data sets only tell an ambiguous tale. However, Moss and Tilly and others (Holzer, 1995; Cappelli, 1996; Murnane and Levy, 1994) contend that basic hard and soft skills are the key skills in question in entry-level jobs and that these skill needs are rising.

INTERVIEW FINDINGS ABOUT CHANGING SKILL REQUIREMENTS FOR ENTRY-LEVEL MANUFACTURING JOBS

The Inclusion of Floor Supervisors into the Interview Process

In these interviews I did not undertake the direct observation of workers that Fernandez feels is necessary to gauge changes in skill requirements on the firm level correctly (although I did casually observe workers at work at all but a few firms); these interviews, however, do include the observations of supervisors who have direct contact with workers.

In their work, Kirschenman and Neckerman (1991a and 1991b), Moss and Tilly (1991b), Holzer (1995), and Wilson (1996) relied solely on the observations of CEOs and heads of personnel. I found that individuals in these roles had little direct contact with workers as they performed their tasks, and sometimes appeared to exaggerate changes in skill requirements.

One example of an apparent schism between the observations of a personnel director and a floor supervisor is found at the Big Three auto manufacturer I interviewed as part of the MCSUI project. When asked about skills required for the job of line operator, the personnel director emphasized computer literacy. He turned on his computer so he could illustrate what sounded like a very detailed and somewhat incomprehensible process that line workers were required to know:

> This is a PFS monitor, OK. And what PFS stands for is Performance Feedback System. Throughout this entire facility at work stations you will find what they call PDP Board. What this monitor tells you and I will relate to you how the worker interfaces with this. For example BR is the full size Ram Pickup Truck. . . . the FP stands for Floor Pan. So if I want to know an hourly count this is how many floor pans on the BR I made each hour. The first hour 48, the second hour 0, the third hour 10, the fourth hour 64, etc. The N Truck stands for the Dakota floor pans, that's how many each hour for the first 6 hours of the shift I made. How many I framed, how many went through the paint shop, how many total trucks I built, how many I OK'ed, and how many I shipped. This gives you audit conditions, this gives you weekly average by day of the week audit conditions, this gives you critical conditions that have been found so far during the shift. . . . The people that are actually assembling them, use PDD as the input information relative to critical conditions, what's shy, what's missing, what needs to be repaired OK. So the computer literacy then is a requirement on our part because if they look at these keys and buttons and stuff they have to know how to do them, they have to know how to understand them.

However, the floor supervisor, when addressing the issue of required skills, said:

> We have what we call a PFS System which basically is not that . . . basically it presses a button and it tells you OK this part goes on this vehicle. The main thing they had to learn how to do is learn how to turn it [the computer] on. . . .

In all, line supervisors at 8 of the 26 firms interviewed as part of my study had opinions about the skills of workers that differed from those of their superiors. Floor supervisors seemed to be a more reliable source about skill demands and worker characteristics. They were also far more able to give information about hiring practices as well as their workers' economic and family backgrounds, methods of transportation to work, and childcare needs.

INTERVIEW FINDINGS: SPECIFIED SKILL
CHANGES IN STUDIED FIRMS

Fewer Firms Report Changing Skill Requirements than Found in Previous Survey Efforts

In keeping with Osterman's findings about the relative lack of skill upgrading in manufacturing firms as compared to firms in other sectors (1995), representatives from only 8 out of the 26 firms I surveyed indicated that they have instituted technical and organizational changes in the last 5 years that have changed task requirements for their respective sample jobs. Representatives from only 5 of these 8 firms indicated that the task changes require more skills from workers than they had in the past; these firms are Mushroom Plastics, Mash Inc., Crowe Products, Satellite Fasteners, and Morgan Stamping.[4]

In addition, there was consensus about this issue among respondents in only 3 of these 5 firms: Mushroom Plastics, Mash Inc., and Crowe Products. On the other hand, the CEO of Satellite Fasteners felt that skill requirements remained unchanged while the floor supervisor said there was an increased need for observational/quality-related skills, and at Morgan Stamping, the CEO felt that the sample job of press operator now actually requires *fewer* skills since they automated the process, while the floor supervisor said it required more skills than in the past.

Respondents from 2 of the 8 firms reporting recently implemented organizational and/or technological changes, other than Morgan Stamping (Twain Plastics and Sergeant Gum) also indicated that technical and organizational changes actually reduced the skills necessary to perform the sample job.

My findings may also be different than those of Holzer and Moss and Tilly, who found far more evidence of increased skill requirements, not only because I focused on the manufacturing sector but also because I attempted to focus on changes in personal qualities among workers demanded by shifts in job content. This was done by asking whether the firms had instituted technical or organizational changes in the past 5 years, how these changes then affected job content, and finally, whether they required a worker with different skills than they had in the past.

The responses of the head of personnel at Planet Products are a good example of an articulation of the difference between a shift in job content and a change in required skills. He stated:

Most of the equipment here is about 5 years old or less, so I mean it is relatively recent-type stuff, high tech, computerized, latest state-of-the-art kind of thing . . . there's definitely a lot more changes in the industry, I mean we are getting more technical as far as with the SPC and you know, the Big Three are basically forcing a lot of people to have statistical programs and become a Q-1 supplier. But as far as changes in people to meet those? No. But again, that Powerway [quality] System is so basic, as long as you have a good Q-C manager or an educated person there to make sure it runs smooth, as far as an operator goes, it's still real simplified.

A Note About SPC and Other Quality Processes

All the firms that were involved with the direct manufacture of products for the auto industry (this excludes the repair shops and propane gas providers) have been required to implement quality control measures by their customers: the Big Three or their first-tier suppliers. The most frequently mentioned skill-related change noted by representatives from these firms is in the institution of statistical process control (SPC), a quality-control mechanism that involves testing (or simply observing) a statistically determined sample of produced parts for defects and charting the results.

Although a few respondents noted the difficulty of this process and considered its implementation to comprise their reported skill change,[5] other respondents said that SPC actually made workers' jobs easier, since this process in many places has been automated along with other functions that were formerly all done by operators on the line. For example, the CEO of Twain Plastics noted:

SPC and things like that have taken, we've hired people to do that, so it's taken some of the requirements from them to check parts and stuff away from them, so the requirement to understand how to do it has been reduced. It opened the door to people that had less skills.

The floor supervisor at Planet Products echoed this observation when he elaborated on task changes in his firm that includes a new emphasis on SPC:

Well, what we've tried to do is take as much out of the workers' hands as possible. So, I mean, what we're really, really looking for is a worker that has common sense, that has the work ethic, again, and wants to build this job into something more than just a line-operator position. The rest of it will take care of itself. Honestly, it really is a very, very easy environment to learn if you have the right skills. And those skills again, I think, are just if you've got the willingness to learn, basic mathematical skills, and open to more education so that you can absorb further training. And we take it from there. Okay?

This response was a variation of "give us someone who has a good attitude and we'll do the rest," reflecting a focus on "soft" rather than "hard" skill requirements that was heard often among respondents in this study as well as those interviewed by researchers conducting similar studies.

Other respondents emphasized that even the most poorly educated worker could learn SPC (if trained). The floor supervisor at Dartmouth Stamping replied when asked whether he has observed problems among in workers in hard skills, like learning SPC:

Well, not really, because I've worked in Detroit most of my life, and my main thing was on the east side of Detroit. We taught people SPC that couldn't even, they'd ask me how much their check was at the end of the week, but they could do SPC and chart and graph, and do it better than somebody with a high school education. It's very easy to teach people that want to work. And you need no education at all, if you know how to count up to 100, you can learn SPC, and you can do charting, that's all there is to it. It's just the way you teach them.

FIVE FIRMS REPORTING CHANGES IN SKILL REQUIREMENTS: MUSHROOM PLASTICS, MASH INC., CROWE PRODUCTS, SATELLITE FASTENERS, AND MORGAN STAMPING

These 5 firms, each of which had representatives who stated that skill needs are increasing, did not present an unequivocal argument for their increasing skill demands. Although 2 of the 3 interviewed white-owned suburban firms are in this subsample of 5 (Mushroom Plastics and Mash Inc.), these firms were among the 4 firms in the total sample where CEOs or heads of personnel blocked interviews with floor supervisors (the others are Sergeant Gum and CalOrange Industries: see table 1-2). Therefore, as in the case of Wilson's or the early Moss and Tilly interviews, the higher-level respondents who were interviewed may be presenting an exaggerated view about whether shifts in job content actually affect the required skills of workers on the factory floor, or they may know more about work processes than floor supervisors.

In addition, the one firm in this group that is fully black-owned and operated—Morgan Stamping—is also the firm where the CEO felt that entry-level jobs had been recently downskilled through increased automation of their metal stamping process, while the relatively newly hired supervisor felt that their work required more skills than in the past.

Whether or not skill requirements were said to have changed, employers sought relatively rudimentary skills. This finding confirms that of Osterman, who noted an increasing gap between the types of skills required by blue- and white-collar jobs (1995). It also confirms recent work of Murnane, who noted that employers tended to state that they were seeking workers with skills at a ninth-grade educational level for entry-level jobs.[6] The questions remains whether even workers who have completed high school possess these skills.

Among the entire sample of 26 firms, no respondent indicated that their entry-level workers needed hard skills that were in excess of those normally gained through an eighth-grade education. The firms that indicated that they require a high school degree (there were only 5),[7] indicated that they do so to assure that applicants have basic reading and math skills. By "basic" math skills, employers said that entry-level workers are required to know how to perform addition, subtraction, multiplication, and division (the most advanced required math skills included knowledge about decimal points and how to use simple measurement tools). "Basic" reading skills were described as literacy—so that workers may read instructions and safety regulations—and "basic" writing skills were described, for example, as the ability to write SPC charts.

Respondents from only two firms said that their sample entry-level job now required more conceptual skills; yet these respondents also note that they are unable to hire applicants who have them. For example, the CEO of Mash Inc. stated that he perceives the increase in skills to center around reasoning and logic skills—what he called "conceptual skills"—that have resulted in his looking for a different sort of machine operator (his plant produced plastic and metal fittings):

> Well, basically in the old days, you would look for somebody who had
> manual dexterity and had the ability I would say to get that glazed look
> in their eyes where they enter their own never-never land and just me-

chanically move a work piece in and out, and that's all they did. . . .
now we're looking for people . . . who can say okay, if something's
going wrong they can tell us about it right away. As I say, they have to
be able to understand, it's pretty complex machines, be able to do a variety of tasks, be able to, gosh, how would you compare it? You know,
they've got to be able to not only program their VCR, they've got to be
able to run their microwave and set the oven to cook the chicken at ten
o'clock tonight, you know? . . . it's a variety of skills and it's their ability to retain these skills and do them efficiently.

However, his search for this type of worker has not been successful
(he is located on the Groesbeck Corridor in Roseville; 91 percent of his
76 machine operators are white). He stated:

A lot of times if you take somebody and you say, this is what I want
you to do, this specific thing, you have to sometimes come back and reinforce it and reinforce it, in part because you're not going to be able to
say, I want you to do this because of this, and they'll pick up the further
information from that, and then you can rely on them. I mean, it's like
sometimes you have to spell out every little thing. So I think that's
what I would say.

This CEO further noted that his hard skill needs include "very basic,
old-time skills. Math, math-based skills, science-based, physical science-based skills. . . . They need to be literate, absolutely. And we need
them to be able to do multiplication, division, addition, subtraction."
Workers do not need to know how to calculate fractions and decimals,
but "would have to know how to write them down."

Similarly, the head of personnel at suburban white-owned Mushroom Inc. noted that "the new ones coming in have to be able to read and
write and do arithmetic because they have to do statistics on their job,
and they have to fill out all kinds of productivity charts, efficiency charts,
scrap charts and things, they have to." She noted that both older long-
time employees as well as many new younger employees "don't have the
skills that the new people I'm currently hiring, that I'm requiring them to
have." She indicated that she is more likely to find these skills among experienced older applicants (who are displaced from previous jobs) than
younger applicants, noting that she was "surprised because I didn't realize that the rates were so high for people that don't finish school or drop
out or they don't go back for their GED."

Most of the younger workers are high school dropouts. She felt that 10 percent of applicants do not have basic reading and math skills. Minority employees in this firm number fewer than 5 percent (as noted in chapter 5, none of the new hires are black, and minority workers date from the time before this personnel director's tenure). Workers in the sample job operate light machinery that either stamps or molds plastic parts.

Employers in the 3 black-owned firms where at least one respondent noted that skill needs have increased are also seeking workers with "basic skills." However, the white floor supervisor at Crowe Products noted that he is selecting people with a knowledge of algebra to head entry-level teams, stating:

> ... well, there's really not a whole lot of math skills involved, because the only thing the guys really do is weigh things up, but we are getting into algebraic formulas now for calculating things such as linear footage, theoretical null weights, so they're coming into effect too. ...

This supervisor characterizes entry-level work as "not hard work but it's continuous fast-paced work. There's a degree of responsibility that is put on every employee." He further stated that he feels the applicant pool has gotten better in recent years:

> Well, basically I think the people are smarter than they used to be. ... I think they're going further in school than they used to, tell you the truth. I think back maybe 10, 15 years ago, maybe even 20 years ago, people were dropping out of school left and right. But I don't think it's as much nowadays as it used to be, I think people are staying in school longer, myself.

Satellite Fasteners and Morgan Stamping are the only two firms in this group of five that require high school degrees; however, the skills they require are very basic. The white floor supervisor at Morgan Stamping stated that: "Yeah, it seems like, well basically, it's really mandatory now that the operators . . . you know, a few years back we had inspectors doing all the work, you know, now it's relied on the operators to do their quality checks, do their own charting, and so forth like that. Yeah, it has changed."

However, the firm's CEO stated that the skills required for the job have lessened due to automation, but an understanding of math is still required (for SPC):

> They're asked to sample parts and come up with an average . . . in order for us to get reporting, it really holds the whole company back if they aren't able to read and write.

This CEO has recently required that applicants have a high school diploma or a GED because she was then "[h]oping that there would be no problems with literacy and basic math, but we find that that's not necessarily the case."

Like the CEO at Mash Inc., the floor manager at Satellite Fasteners puts less emphasis on math and writing skills (although workers need both) and stressed conceptual, quality-oriented skills:

> . . . the demands of the customer require that the operator be more familiar and more technical with the part he is making, such as drain flows in the steel, they got to be aware of how they are making this part now. In the old days, they just stamped them out, but now the quality requirements are way higher.

As mentioned, this firm's CEO disagreed that skill requirements have changed in the past 5 years, though he stressed the need both for basic math and reading skills. However, he appeared not to put as much emphasis on formal qualifications as his floor supervisor, noting:

> Here is the person that comes in that has 20 years in a header shop that knows the equipment. He don't have the education, or he has problems with his math, and that. And, everything else is in line, the attitude, the willingness to work, and that. We will take that individual and work with him in those areas where he is short. Okay?

In other words, they will train someone with a poor educational background who is willing to be trained and who, as so many say, "has the right attitude and a good work ethic," the "soft" skills which most interviewed employers note are the most valued skills of all.

As authors like Osterman and Fernandez have stressed, these responses appear to underscore that changing technology may create shifts in job content for entry-level workers, yet there does not appear to be a clear consensus about whether hard skill needs are increasing for entry-level jobs.

Hard skill changes that were described ranged from no skills required at all (other than physical endurance) to the requirement of very basic reading and math skills. As noted, respondents from only two firms noted an increased need for conceptual skills.

However, these findings do not contradict the literature that documents the overall decease in these types of jobs, and the downshift in wages paid for relatively unskilled jobs compared to jobs requiring more skills in this and other sectors. Since African Americans are disproportionately concentrated in lower-skilled jobs, the wage and employment ramifications are obvious. Yet wage shifts between greater- and lesser-skilled workers neither provide an explanation for why the black-owned firms pay lower wages nor why white-owned suburban firms pay comparatively high wages even in comparison to white-owned firms in the city of Detroit. It is these issues that the subsequent sections of the chapter address.

Until this point, this chapter has primarily focused on hard skills such as math and literacy. As previously noted, authors such as Wilson and Moss and Tilly have hypothesized that perhaps it is not just a comparative lack of hard skills that is holding black workers back from making continuing gains in employment and wages; instead, black applicants may be especially lacking in soft skills such as interpersonal skills and positive work attitudes, in a time when there may be an increasing emphasis on such skills in the labor market. This notion is more fully explored in the sections below, where employers' perceptions of both hard and soft skill needs, and whether there are perceived differences among whites and blacks, are compared. The chapter concludes with a focus on skill needs and worker characteristics among the three highest-paying white-owned firms in this sample and their low-paying matches.

EMPLOYER PERCEPTIONS OF RACIAL AND/OR LOCATIONALLY-BASED SKILL DIFFERENCES AMONG WORKERS

Racial Differences

I had extended conversations with nearly all of the 51 respondents about perceived racial and/or locational skill differences (see Appendix B for summaries).[8] Of the 44 people who addressed racial differences, 25 (or

56 percent) stated that they saw no differences between the skills (both hard and soft) of white and black workers. Interestingly, there appears to be very little difference among white and black respondents in regard to this issue: the percentage breakdown is almost the same. Ten out of 17 (or 58 percent) of the African-American respondents felt there were no racially determined skill differences among their workers, while slightly fewer whites (15 out of 27, or 55 percent) expressed similar views.

Nearly all of the 19 respondents who saw skill differences among workers noted that that these differences were in the realm of hard skills. Unlike the findings reported in previous studies (i.e., Kirschenman and Neckerman, 1991b; Moss and Tilly, 1991b; Wilson, 1996), where employers reported that African-American workers in general (and black men in particular) had poor work attitudes, only 4 respondents from this effort felt that the attitudes of black workers were inferior to those of whites. Two of these were white female personnel officers commenting on what they considered to be the poor attitudes of black men; two male supervisors—one black male and one white—felt similarly.

However, four additional respondents actually felt that black workers had *better* soft skills than white workers: they said that African-American workers worked harder, and had greater motivation and better attitudes than white workers (one of these respondents was the white floor supervisor from Sears Inc., a low-wage black-owned firm; another was a white supervisor at Planet Products, which offers a mid-range starting wage; the other two were the black CEO and director of personnel from the low-wage black-owned firm Silver, Inc.).

Spatial Differences

To address whether there might be locationally based determinants of skill differences aside from race, respondents were asked to compare the skills of blacks and whites from the city to both blacks and whites from the suburbs: for example, "do you think that the skills of blacks from the suburbs more closely resemble those of suburban whites or city blacks, etc." Most respondents (particularly city African-American employers) felt that they could not answer skill/location questions since they had never employed suburban blacks and/or city whites—an interesting finding in itself.

However, 16 respondents reported that they perceived locational differences that superseded racial considerations; this number included 11 city white employers, 2 suburban white employers, and 3 black respondents (2 city and one suburban). Ten of these employers also noted racially determined skill differences as well. Finally, 7 respondents pointed out that the skills of white suburban workers were thought to be especially poor, especially among workers who lived in more economically disadvantaged suburbs.

The remainder of this chapter focuses on the comments of respondents who perceived racially or locationally determined skill differences, in order to get a sense of their nature and extent. I only briefly address the comments of those who did not see such differences among workers. The final section of this chapter compares the three highest-paying (white-owned) firms and their black-owned low-paying matches to evaluate whether increased skill requirements and/or race or locationally based skill differences among workers could be a factor in the documented wage differences among sampled white- and black-owned firms.

PERCEIVED RACIAL DIFFERENCES

Black Respondents

Most of the seven black employers who noted racially determined skill differences sought to connect their observations about these differences to larger social and economic issues, rather than focusing on the personal deficiencies of workers. The CEO of Cannon Chemical described why he thought skill differences between blacks and whites existed and persisted; he also took the role of the white employer to explain the erosion of black economic gains. He was also one of the three African-American owners who refused to differentiate between location and race as determinants of skill differences.

He noted that "urban problems are the same" for whites and blacks. Since the city of Detroit is largely black, and the suburbs are overwhelmingly white, he asked: "[H]ow are those different? . . . first of all, I don't see those as being different, okay?" After first attributing differences in skills between city and suburban employees to an interaction of poor schools and disrupted family life, he later moved from the family as the nexus of success or failure for a particular urban child to larger societal issues, such as spatial polarization and the economic abandonment of Detroit:

> Well, if there is a thing called race, okay, and if all the negatives that go along with racial inferiority are there, then by definition when you add

skills and ability to that, okay, you don't see that black person as having the same skills and ability as that white person. . . . to the extent
that we are separated in terms of where we live and we are separated in
terms of the way we appear to each other, that's a factor that is
there. . . . I mean obviously when you find that there are more African-
Americans in jail than in college, that tells you, African American
males probably, that tells you an awful lot about what's going on on the
employment side.

He had a clear grasp of the theory of spatial mismatch without actually using the term:

The other side, if you take a look at simply the demographics of
where blacks are, where jobs are, if you find that there's a huge
growth of employment in the suburbs and that as you take a look at
where the opportunities for growth have been, where companies have
placed themselves, okay, they've placed themselves outside of urban
centers. So once you're outside the area where people can be trans-
ported to get those particular jobs, obviously the center city starts
wanting. And a city like Detroit that's literally had no growth . . . it's
not difficult to find out that obviously there's been no employment
growth in the city.

As discussed in more detail later in this chapter, this CEO was not
unhappy with the skills and abilities of his largely black production
workforce; he did not have difficulty locating workers with adequate
skills (although many applicants fail the drug screen), and his turnover
was very low.

Other black employers who perceived skill differences between
black and white workers cited educational differences as an explanation
for them. For example, the CEO of Woodward Gas, who has operations
both in the city of Detroit and the middle-class white suburb of Novi,
first indicted the suburban school system for what he sees as the deteriorating skills among white suburban youth:

. . . they're not being taught in school. They're not being taught, they're
not being challenged, they're not being taught how to think. Kids don't
think [in Novi and Southfield]. . . . They don't have the ability to reason or to come to a conclusion, given a set of problems they cannot de-
duce the answer from that.

Yet when asked to compare city and suburban schools in more detail, he stated that city schools are worse: "[the] Detroit school system is not producing the actual skills to the same degree. The kids from Novi have the skills, but they don't have the reasoning ability, but the kids from Detroit, they don't have the skills or the reasoning ability, so they are doubly handicapped."

The black president of Sears Metals also noted that black workers have less hard skills than white workers (she also noted that she has no black workers from the suburbs or white workers from the city). She stated that white applicants tend to have more technical skills; "I think it's from the education, background that they've experienced"; she also perceived "minor" racial differences in ability to fill out application forms. She did not see racial differences in work ethic or attitude: "I've had experience with both. I mean, how are you going to say something if you really haven't experienced it? I try to stick to what I've experienced."

The CEO of Twain Plastics, while denigrating the skills of his nearly 100 percent black workforce, was just as quick to note that he considered educational disparities of the city and suburban schools as the most obvious indication of racial discrimination in society and the key reason for perceived skill differences between blacks and whites, as well as their eroding economic gains:

> ... there's clearer levels of discrimination. The society is far more discriminatory today than it has ever been in my lifetime. . . . When I can look at the disparity between the school systems, and as an employer I can see it. And as a parent I can see it.

He further noted that city and suburban school systems are as different as "night and day. You could take the absolute honor roll student in the city, they would have a hard time competing against a suburban student. Probably couldn't compete."

This observation that a high school education for the typical black student is inferior than that offered to suburban whites echoes the suggestion of Newman and Stack that the quality of education between racial groups may be different enough to cause human capital differences between blacks and whites (1992). Differences in educational quality between black and white school districts are later described by white respondents in this sample, although a few believe that the quality of education offered by both the city and surrounding lower-to-middle-income white suburbs is equally bad.

Only one black respondent noted that although he perceived no differences between black and white workers in hard skill attainment, he did see racial differences in work ethic and attitude: this was the black floor supervisor at Lionel Plastics, a black-owned suburban firm producing plastic machined parts. He stated that the work ethic of young workers of any race

> is not like mine was. Mine was, they tell me to do a job, then boom, that was it. I would do the job. I would go to it and I would give it my best. With me, I just do my job, and I do it the best I could. But a lot of them now, they get on there, they don't want to do it. "Why, I gotta go here . . . why I gotta," you know.

He felt that this attitude is more prevalent among young blacks: "I have to lean toward it's more towards the black, because everyone that I had to deal with [discipline], it was a black. You know, I know it's bad to say, but I'm being truthful." He felt this is a result of blacks feeling as though they are being taken advantage of (the workforce in this black-owned suburban firm is still 65 percent white): "[M]y opinion is that they feel that the white person is being allowed to do just about basically what they want to do, and where they want to go, okay. And, whereas the black person feel that they getting put over here because they're black or this or that . . . ."

The supervisor at Lionel felt that black workers have the same opportunities in this firm as whites, but still "they feel like someone, they're just singling them out, you know." He felt that these poor attitudes are only prevalent among black men. He stated: "I believe because a lot of these (black) women got a lot of us black men spoiled . . . like I say, a lot of them are used to depending on a black woman where they support them, okay."[9]

This floor supervisor also felt that suburban whites have bad attitudes:

> . . . a lot of them come from around here, a lot are from the suburbs, and it seems like they don't really have to work, they're just here. . . . when they hire in, it's just like, you know, they don't have to work. Because we had some guys come in and they say, well I don't need this, and they will work on a certain job for a while. And we have some just walk on off and leave, you know," [while young black workers] try to stick it out, but eventually they don't walk off. They just might not come back [the next day].

The head of operations at Curve-All described many differences in hard and soft skills among black and white workers, but did not attempt to determine reasons for this outside of their personal characteristics. He stated, after speaking at length of how important a good education is to work success, that the Detroit schools are "terrible" because "a school or institution, I always feel, is who's there." Yet later in the interview, he stated:

> Let's face it, this city was let go for a long time. You know, it just needs a total revitalization, vitalizing of everything, you know. Get the city together. I know it sounds easy and simple, but things need to get better, people need to start working for continuous improvement, you know. And it starts from home, city, your work environment. You know, it doesn't have to be this way.

Even when addressing the deterioration of the city of Detroit, this operations head still couched his perceptions in what appears to be what he considered are clear differences between blacks and whites. When asked about the skills and abilities of city whites, he said:

> But overall, my perception is that normally, white people generally do better. And you know, the way I look at it, from going to college and high school and all that, I've gone through predominantly, the college I went to was only 5 percent minority, and the high school I went to, there was 1,000 kids or so, and only a handful of blacks. . . . But I always saw, seems like white people generally came from good families, and most of my roommates at school, they all, they seemed to just have basic necessities for a foundation for a positive life. . . . Then I look around at minorities, and it just seems like blacks, you see a lot more of the opposite. Like the focus and effort isn't there.

White Respondents

All but a few of the 12 white respondents who noted differences in skills between white and black workers focused on hard skills; for example, the head of personnel at Planet Products stated:

> I think the skills are deteriorating, personal feeling, for the community [Detroit]. The skills are much, much weaker in the community . . . there is a fear of math. Reading, not to a certain extent, although the

reading that we require is interpretation of part numbers, sequential lot numbering, those types of thing which are just kind of common sense to the average person, I see that some workers tend to have a real hard time capturing that, okay.

He further stated that he now sees less motivation and leadership potential among black workers than he had seen in the past:

I've had some black workers come in and again, show the motivation and show the interest and be able to train properly, and I've had some that aren't. It's kind of, I keep saying 50-50, but I really do see that I'm getting some, because I'm keeping some, as you can see I've got 40 percent [black workers] here, so I'm keeping some, but I'm just not seeing that spark, that talent that puts that black worker over and above where he could be trained for a leadership role.

The floor manager at Planet came to his plant after a long stint at an all-white plant located in the downriver community of Melvindale, which is a lower-income, blue-collar suburb. Like the personnel director, he also noted hard skill differences between black and white workers at Planet; but unlike the personnel director, he thought that black workers have better work attitudes and ethics than white workers. Early in the interview he stated:

Here I think their skills are less than that of downriver. . . . It could be how much school they did accomplish. At Winchell's [the downriver plant] you've probably got a little bit more of people who went to school longer. Down here, boy it's really hard, if it was really up to me I wouldn't even accept applications from down here . . . half of them that are down here are living in homeless shelters or they're coming out of drug programs, which, and I've tried those people and I thought they might work out. You know, this is a second chance, these guys are going to go, but it doesn't work out.

He finally stated:

I think as far as the employees here in Detroit, [they are] much harder workers than downriver workers . . . at Winchells's as far as plating goes, there's probably 70 percent efficient, versus 85 to 90 percent efficient here. . . . I know that kind of does sound awful strange [that he

later states that black workers have better work ethics after earlier noting that he would not hire them if he could get away with it]. And I
don't know, maybe that's my inner fear with the city, I don't know. . . .
I think I want the mentality of the downriver people but I want the
work ethics of these people.

The white floor supervisor at minority-owned Sears Metals had similar views about better work ethics among black workers, and he also felt
that on an overall basis, hard skills are improving among the applicant
pool of black workers: "I'm seeing more people that have gone back and
gotten their GED now than ever before. I used to get a lot of applications
from people that had never finished school. Now I'm seeing a lot more of
that now." Furthermore, he noted that:

> . . . in the past 5 years, I think the black people that I have hired, it
> seems like they want to work harder than the whites I've seen. But,
> then again, like I said, that might not be fair because, you drive around
> here, and the majority of the people you see are going to be black.

He attributed what he considered to be worse hard skills among
blacks, along with their perceived greater willingness to work hard, to
the economic abandonment of Detroit, and the spatial polarization of
whites and blacks:

> Well, I think a lot of your higher paying jobs are out of the city, and a
> majority of your white people, seem like they live outside the city. And
> maybe that's why. I think you're less apt to get into trouble living out-
> side the city because of the problems with the gangs are happening,
> and everything else. It just seems like. I've had this opinion for a cou-
> ple of years. It seems to me like, I would hate to be, not necessarily a
> young black kid, but any kid, high school kid, growing up in the city
> right now. Because it just seems like they don't have a chance to get
> ahead because they're living, it seems like they're constantly living in a
> tough situation. I think that's why you see a lot of people moving out of
> the city, just to get away from it, but it's following them. Sooner or
> later, they're going to have to face the fact that they've got to take care
> of theirselves [*sic*], and that you can't run away from it.

Finally, the floor supervisor at Dartmouth Stamping reported that he
thought that there were clear differences in motivation between black

and white workers (although he later admitted that he thought that black workers learned faster on the job than white workers):

> I think the attitude now [in plants], who works harder, black or white? Well, whites do. There's no question about it. As a whole. As individuals, you've got blacks that will tear up a white guy, and I've got whites that will tear up a black guy. As a whole, whites work harder. And that is, that's the mind-set in the industry.

Although many white city respondents were sensitive to some of the educational and personal disadvantages that black workers must contend with, most black employers were better able to articulate the varied social, spatial, and economic factors that contribute to their perceptions of skill differences of black and white workers. In addition, in contrast to findings from earlier interview studies, very few respondents of either race noted racially determined skill differences in work ethic and attitude. The concern and focus was on hard skill differences, even though most interviewed employers indicated that a good work attitude was perhaps the most important skill sought.

PERCEIVED LOCATIONAL DIFFERENCES

Employers also perceived differences in the skills and abilities of workers based on where they live. The focus of this section is on how employers perceive differences between the skills and abilities of city whites and blacks and suburban whites and blacks. Sixteen employers specifically noted that city workers and suburban workers had different skills and abilities, regardless of their race. These included 13 white and 3 African-American respondents.[10]

Black-owned Firms

One of the 3 African-American employers who noted locational differences in skills among workers stressed the fact that because the city of Detroit is home to 80 percent of the region's black population, while the surrounding suburban population is only 7 percent black, race is easily equated with space. When asked whether he saw differences in quality for black and white applicants, or differences in skills and abilities between city and suburban residents, the CEO of Twain Plastics replied: "I think I see it more between the city and suburban than black or white."

However, when asked whether perceived differences were more locational than racial, he stated:

> That wouldn't be fair because geography also determines what the race is. Okay, it's like saying I got all the women living in Ann Arbor and all the men living in East Lansing, is there a sexual difference between the two campuses? And no, it's geographical.

This CEO, who would rather talk race than space, still noted that in the past 5 years, city applicants have become "less polite, less aware what it takes to get a job. Absolutely less direction." He felt this change in quality is equally true for black and white applicants, if

> you find the same type of inner-city area. I think it's more true for blacks because they tend to centralize around a city area more than the whites, as far as a percentage base. They suffer from the same kind of problems. And when I'm saying inner city, you go out to Warren [a white low-income suburb where two of the white-owned high-paying firms in this sample are located] and places like that, you run into the same type of problems . . . in Warren, it's incredible. Lots of lost souls in Warren.

The CEO of Silver Inc. first addressed what he perceived to be the reaction of young black urban residents to their disenfranchisement from the expectations and demands of the working world, and how white employers may perceive them:

> Especially with the youth, they're angry . . . and then they're coming up through a system that guarantees failure for them. And then they strike out and try to be applicants for jobs and they don't realize that they're light years behind the eight ball. But bigger than that is that they often feel that after a year of searching, or two years of searching, they give up. And then they say the system's failed them. Black-youth males are very angry and very frightening to the average employer.

Yet Silver did not see differences of the skills and abilities of black and white applicants that he interviews for jobs in his city-based plant. He noted:

I don't think it [race] makes any difference. I think if they're in the same economic boat, you get about the same employee. He may talk different, but that's just about it. Their value systems are the same. One thing I can tell you about young white males that I've noticed in probably 15 years, is they're very easily content, the ones I've seen. They'll get a job and you never hear from them again. Whereas a black guy, if I go out in the shop and he's right in my face, you know, "Mr. Silver, do you think I can get this job, or do you think I can get that?" The white, and maybe because the company is just more black than white, they play a fading role.

When seeking an explanation for what he considered to the be the greater motivation of his black workers, he noted:

I think also that they obviously feel that they can talk to me because I'm of the same race, and maybe the white doesn't think so. So I, you know, like I said, that situation could be totally reversed in another company. It's funny, I've had some employees 18 and 19 years, to watch them change from these fireballs that are just their own biggest problem into someone who now realizes that the only person who's going to take care of him is himself!

This observation about comfort levels between employers and workers of the same race may also be an explanation of why white employers may see less motivation among black workers in majority-white plants. Silver also noted that both black suburban applicants and workers come across very differently than either black or white city residents, which he attributed to the better environment and schools found in the suburbs:

They have better skills. They have a different perceived image of themselves, too. Well, they weren't raised in the, I don't want to say ghetto environment. . . . They were raised in an environment where they had to meet a standard that you don't have in an inner-city school. A 100 percent black school has no standard in some cases. . . . The PTA may be weak. The teachers are weak, the administration is weak, and their whole thing is to cattle shuffle these kids through. Just promote them till they're out. And to me that's nothing, that's absolutely, totally nothing!

The young floor supervisor at Twain Plastics had similar views about black suburbanites:

> I notice that it seems like the suburban blacks come in more of an ea-
> gerness and ready to work attitude, whereas the city, it doesn't really
> make them a difference, it's like they're really killing time and they
> come in like you owe them. Why do you make me fill this application
> out, and fool, you should just hire me.

After stating that he felt that city whites were more apt to resemble their black urban counterparts than white suburbanites, he offered this explanation:

> Because in the city it's more of a fast type of life, a lot of noise, more
> people, the morals and principles are different. In the city neighbor-
> hood there's loud music, people are up at all times of the night. The
> suburbs is basically quiet, kind of peaceful. You have to find your own,
> you have to find ways to entertain yourself in the suburbs whereas in
> the city you just roll your window up. Just pull the shade up and look
> out.

He later added that city residents appear to lack role models:

> It starts out at an early age but before you know it you're a grown adult
> and you have no idea how to pay bills, how to manage money and fi-
> nances, how to acquire a house, haven't developed any type of skills
> that's actually marketable for yourself to get a good job or a position
> somewhere in a company. And in your mind, you have fixed thoughts
> that this is the way it is and this is the way it's going to be until I die,
> so . . . and then you've got the streets that's dictating their direction. So
> therefore a mass amount of young blacks aren't seeking employment,
> aren't seeking any skills to become employed, because they're letting
> the streets dictate their finances and how they do things.

White Respondents

The theme that both black and white city residents resembled each other in their abilities and skills because they were isolated and defeated was also one that was prevalent among white respondents who noted differ-ences in city and suburban residents that transcended race. For example, the floor manager at Planet Products noted that city residents are dealing on a 24-hour basis with issues that he found overwhelming as a commuter; consequently, he stated that he understood the lack of motivation that he saw among both black and white Detroiters:

> I didn't know if I was going to be able to handle this area [Detroit—he is from the downriver suburb of Melvindale] because, it all goes back like when I worked in Melvindale, your typical excuse is for a line operator might have been oh, I was sick today or my car wouldn't start. Now I get excuses like, well, my pit bull attacked my neighbor's pit bull and he shot my house up last night. Or, you know, my sister's boyfriend caught her with another man and he shot her right through the chest, you know. A lot of violence and it really is a lot of violence down there . . . just talking to the people, cause it's really so hard to deal with this, it's everyday life for them. . . . Yeah, I'm off of work and I'm going home, can you imagine going home to a house that don't even have windows on it? Why should you care about what you're doing in that plant if that's what you're going home to? I wouldn't care.

Other white employers felt that black and white Detroiters have hard skills that are not as good as those of suburbanites, but Detroiters possess better interpersonal skills and are more racially tolerant. For example, the CEO at Maybee Industries noted:

> I think they're much more, maybe they've been always forced into that interaction, where maybe a lot of people here have grown up in their little neighborhoods. But the floor level, where it's much more central Detroit, they're much more used to that cultural diversity in Detroit. See, I guess I could generalize things, the people who work down on the floor here, on the entry level, live closer to here. So obviously, they live in proximity, which gives them more cultural diversity. The more professional we get, the more our backgrounds become homogeneous, okay, and maybe the less tolerant they are.

Like his boss, the floor supervisor at Maybee felt that city whites and blacks have the same skills and abilities as each other, although he noted that there are few blacks among his skilled workers. He stated: "I think the majority though of white workers are from the city of Detroit. Basic skills, even up through the skilled level, I have, they seem, my black workers seem to be as equally skilled as any white workers that I have." He also noted that dismissal rates are the same for blacks and whites, and that both groups have drug problems (the main reason for dismissal). Like most other white Detroit employers, he blamed the environment of Detroit for fostering these problems, and said it does not matter if the residents are black or white:

> Sure, because I think what's happened is they've seen the city deteriorate, they've seen their own lives deteriorate to the point that the city affects them, they are living in a lousy neighborhood, I think it takes a lot of their personal gain, or their personal attitude towards personal gain away. . . . But I do think that the decay of the city has a lot to do with it.

These "neighborhood effects" have been discussed, but are often disputed in the literature (see Mayer and Jencks, 1989; Cutler and Glaeser, 1995) because they are so difficult to measure objectively. A supervisor in a downtown drugstore that I interviewed as part of the MCSUI effort summed up what he considered to be a "sense of hopelessness" among Detroit low-income residents by saying: "[T]he environmental breakdown" also causes "a lack of enthusiasm or lack of accomplishment." He felt that the "work ethic from the basic home training is not there" because "society has turned its back on the lower-income people; their struggle to survive basically is taught too early and that's all they worry about and that's all they care about . . . day-to-day and they don't look beyond that point. I see it with young people . . . there is no thought to buying a home . . . it's basic needs and basic everyday survival. . . . " It is also important to note that this employer was not talking about African Americans specifically, but all Detroit-city residents in general.

Conclusion: Perceived Racial and Locational
Skill Differences between Blacks and Whites

Waldinger found a similarity between employers' views of the work attitudes of less-skilled, entry-level whites and blacks. He writes that the employers he interviewed were less likely to view white workers through the "rose-tinted glasses" that Kirschenman and Neckerman and Moss and Tilly report. Instead:

> A theme of convergence of black and white, not detected by other researchers, also came up in interviews, and this got expressed in a vari-

ety of ways . . . "blacks I've hired are indistinguishable from white workers" (this owner pointed to the higher rate of education among blacks). Blacks are seen as having higher aspirations; blacks are striving. Many are interested in higher positions and promotions. Most of the immigrants are not . . . Black men—even American white men—they say "I'm not going to wash dishes" or they'll say, "I went to high school and I deserve better" (1993).

As reported in the opening of this chapter section, a majority of employers (both black and white) in this survey reported, like the employers Waldinger interviewed, that white workers who applied for entry-level factory jobs had poor skills that differed little from those of black workers. Several employers additionally pointed out that all of their applicants, regardless of their race or place of residence, had deteriorating and/or poor skills.

However, when looking at the totality of respondents, a clear majority (32 out of 44, or 72 percent) felt that they could perceive skill differences between black and white and/or city and suburban workers. Respondents were most likely to see these differences as a response to the different characteristics of where workers live, particularly reflected in what many consider to be the comparatively poor education received in the school districts in Detroit. Economic and social differences expressed spatially are said to contribute more to skill differences than the worker's race per se.

As Wilson and others have noted, one need not be black to suffer the ill-effects of economic and social isolation (Wilson, 1987; Newman and Stack, 1992). However, a key concern of this study is whether the average black applicant has skill levels that are different enough from those of the average white applicant to provide a basis for the prevalence of statistical discrimination on the part of employers, and/or to explain the difference in wages and employment among owners with largely white or largely black workforces.

In this sample, at least, among these employers, perceived skill differences between either black and white and/or city and suburban workers are minor. Only one employer described a lack of skills among black workers as a serious problem (Curve-All: a firm that appeared to have many problems in addition to a lack of worker skills). There were white employers who felt that their white workers lacked skills (e.g., the supervisor at Lackwanna; the CEO at Maybee; the floor supervisor at Dartmouth). Other employers noted how skill levels among black workers appeared to be increasing (the supervisor at Sears Metals, the supervisor at Morgan Stamping, and the directors of personnel at Silver and Lionel, among others).

However, the *perception* that more significant skill differences exist between whites and blacks may still be a factor in the higher wages offered in the higher-paying suburban firms surveyed here; it is noteworthy that white employers in the firms (including Mushroom Products, Janis Snap and Tool, and Mash, Inc.) who report that they could not address race or locational issues because they did not employ enough black and/or city residents to form an opinion, all noted that their white workers had poor skills.

The failure to find a clear consensus among interviewed employers for race-based skill differences does not mean that, on a more regional or national basis, differences in skills between blacks and whites do not contribute to growing gaps in employment and wages seen at these levels of study. In addition, the manufacturing firms that participated in this study, as a group, demand few skills. As Osterman and others have noted, other sectors of employers may require more skills than are easily obtained in an urban setting, and skill differences between blacks and whites (and/or urban and suburban residents) may be more apparent. To get a better sense of this issue, I compare the stated skill requirements and employer perceptions of their workforces of relatively high-paying firms and their low-paying matches.

LACKAWANNA CHEMICAL AND CANNON CHEMICAL, JANIS AND LIONEL, MUSHROOM PLASTICS AND ELIZABETH PLASTIC PRODUCTS

This chapter section examines whether increased (or greater) skill demands of the job, and the resultant skill characteristics of workers hired for them, may explain higher wages. This question has been examined by various authors who have noted that the wage gap between workers of different skill levels is increasing and other researchers have noted that wage levels appear to be increasingly set apart from skill concerns (Levy, Murnane, and Chen, 1993).[11]

Based on the information offered by employers, there appears to be little difference in either required skill needs or the perceived skill characteristics of workers in higher-paying firms and their lower-paying matches.[12]

Lackawanna Chemical and Cannon Chemical

Lackawanna Chemical and Cannon Chemical are well-matched firms. Both produce specialty chemicals for the auto industry; paint coatings are the primary products of the studied divisions of each firm. Lackawanna Chemical is located in northeast Detroit, about a mile from Cannon Chemical. Lackawanna Chemical and Cannon are small facilities—only 7 workers are at Lackawanna; there are 8 at Cannon. Both facilities are part of much larger corporations. Lackawanna Chemical has a longer history than Cannon Chemical—it has been in production since 1900, and was sold to its second owner in 1958. Fifty people worked at the site until 1982; until this time it was a unionized firm that was 50 percent black.

In 1982 the owner ostensibly shut down the plant to get rid of the union, but then sold this business instead. The present owners, who also own a similar but larger and newer plant in the city of Romulus (20 minutes west of Detroit) reopened with 7 new employees in 1984. The plant's production manager reported that production has gone up 600 percent in the past 10 years. Unbeknownst to him, representatives from the parent corporation reported that they soon planned to shut down the Detroit facility in favor of the Romulus plant.

This firm ties with Janis Snap and Tool as the best-paying firm among all of those studied. It starts workers at $10.00/hour. Average wages are $13.00/hour. All 7 workers at Lackawanna Chemical are white and all live in the suburbs (which may be a selection effect: they can afford to live in the suburbs). For the purposes of this chapter, I focus on the responses of the plant manager, rather than those of the CEO and head of personnel from the parent corporation, who are located some distance away at company headquarters in the Detroit suburb of Southfield. Not only do they have little actual contact with workers at the Detroit facility, but they have also been with the firm for less than 5 years.

The plant manager did not believe that his firm is offering relatively high wages: "We've been using $10 an hour [as a starting wage] for the 9 years I've been here." He said that the work in his plant (as a paint mixer—the sample job) requires few skills:

> [The work is] really broken down into different categories, but I mean they could be easily interchanged. But the skills that I look for, even just the basic, they've got to be able to add, and I'm getting this crude,

I'm sure you've dealt with this . . . They've got to know what a half of
something is, what about a quarter is . . . I'm going to need a half gal-
lon of this or a half pound of this or a half pound of this. Obviously
you're adding fractions when you put the two together and get a pound.
So there's some of that, that goes on, which I don't think they realize
but they're actually doing it anyway.

As for reading skills, Lackawanna's plant manager stated that workers only need to know enough for "day-to-day operation, getting the
work done, associations, I mean I hate to make it as crude as possible,
simple, simple stuff like that. You know, we use codes, which is why they
started the codes. We have a chemical and the agreement might be C-18
or CH-18, associate the two together." He noted that he is not employing
any illiterate workers now (although he did in the past), but that his
workforce has poor reading and writing skills; they have particular difficulty with both reading and verbal comprehension:

But really, for what I would want, and I really haven't achieved this,
okay, and this is reading and communication skills, which the communication starts to cause problems because when you explain rules and
regulations. I have this problem with workers. You know, I'm sort of
diverging a little bit, but as it comes to me . . . But I have a problem
(with) people comprehending what has been told to them with respect
to regulatory, regulations training. And I think this is a problem indus-
trywide, because I talk to other people. We train, we train and the comprehension is almost zip.

Lackawanna's suburban-dwelling workers are all in their early thirties
(one is 23). The plant manager noted that the workforce is all white because the company exclusively hires by word of mouth. He noted "[T]here
is a black guy that's on layoff right now that when he first started working
with the company in 1984, but when I first started working here, there was
two black guys, two white guys, myself. Both those gentlemen retired.
And the rest of the hires have really come through personal contacts."
    The firm does not have any minimum educational requirements.
However, the plant manager prefers to hire high school graduates: not
because the job requires skill levels beyond the ninth grade, but

for the reason that there's enough labor out there, unskilled labor,
where you can afford to be a little pickier, and high school, although
it's not that complicated to finish, it shows that you finished something.

He also noted that recent technical and organizational changes that were implemented to ensure further product quality have not changed the requirements for the type of worker they seek.

The plant manager also said he has few problems with work ethic and attitudes among his workers. He does not have attendance problems because: "I've gone with a smaller crew and more of a flexible working schedule. Essentially, we have a job to do, we have to get it done, and then we can go. It works out pretty good because we usually finish in about seven and a half hours. Sometimes better, sometimes more." He did note that "sometimes I've run into problems where, you know, you give them an inch, they'll take a mile? I don't care if you come in 5 minutes late, next it's 10 minutes late, next it's a half-hour late, tell them to get back, which frustrates the heck out of me, cause you've got to tell them. You'll see that inching in, all the grace period that's allowed. And that's about the only problem that I run into."

In sum, the relatively highly paid workers at Lackawanna Chemical, all of whom are white, are described as having rudimentary skills. The plant manager's primary problem with his workers is their poor communication and comprehension skills, a deficit that white employers often mention black workers having as a result of communicating in "black English."[13] The manager considered the relatively high wages they pay (as well as his generous formal and informal benefits) to be a deterrent to turnover and attitude problems.

As noted, Cannon Chemical's workforce is 100 percent black, while Lackawanna Chemical's is 100 percent white. As shown in chapter 4, Cannon Chemical offers starting wages that are 35 percent below those of Lackawanna Chemical ($6.50 versus $10.00); there is also a 38 percent average wage gap ($8.00 versus $13.00). Benefits for both firms are both excellent, with Lackawanna offering a slightly better package (e.g., more personal days, flexibility for vacation time—see Appendix A). Cannon Chemical's CEO noted that he had few problems with worker skills, but that he has to do quite a bit of screening to get the workers he wants, primarily because so many applicants fail their drug screens, although some "don't meet the verbal and mathematical requirements." He noted that "we wait until we get what we want, so everyone here meets our standard." He stressed the importance of the drug screen:

> Our concern always is that since you're working around hazardous materials, okay, and you're working around equipment and machinery, and you're driving things like high-los and trucks and things of this particular type, our concern is that obviously if you are impaired be-

cause of drug use, then you pose a great risk to the rest of the work-force here and to our very well-being as a company.

Hard skill requirements appear be a bit more demanding at Cannon than at Lackawanna Chemical. Cannon's CEO noted that workers

> have to take inventory, they've got to do things that involve mathematical calculations in terms of checking on the batches that we, that are sent out by our laboratory. There are all kinds of things that they do that require these kinds of skills. We don't expect them to have experience, but we do expect them to have basic skills. . . . we're not talking about advanced math, we're talking read and write and arithmetic here, okay? And I am guessing that someone who has, even if they've graduated, if they were tested at probably 10th or 11th grade, that would be sufficient. We're not looking for a world-beater here, we're looking for guys who can do some very basic things, and who've got good work ethics and good habits and what have you. . . . we're doing a lot of physical kinds of things in terms of moving these chemicals around . . . the environment that you're working in is one in which I guess if I want to define it better I would simply say that it is not wonderful work.

However, unlike the plant manager at Lackawanna Chemical, Cannon's CEO had no complaints about the skills or work attitudes of his workers, saying that he "personally gets the impression overall that the level of skill and the quality of the worker over there is probably higher [here] than it is in my other companies. . . . I find out that for some reason we do have a number of kids over there who have some education beyond high school, okay?"

In addition, Cannon's CEO noted that turnover is low and that he had few problems with workers' work ethic or attitude. The ages of the workers at Cannon Chemical are similar to those of workers at Lackawanna Chemical: the Nigerian floor supervisor noted that "half are young [in their late twenties] and then two are in the early forties."

Janis and Lionel

Janis Snap and Tool is located in Roseville in the Groesbeck Corridor. It was not a perfect match for Lionel Plastics, for its products are metal and not plastic; but the work processes appear to be comparable. The entry-level sample job is that of a maintenance worker who is hired to be trained to become a machine operator. The firm has 75 employees. Operator-trainees start at \$10.00/hour. The average wage for a machine operator is \$11.00-\$12.50/hour. ’

I was able to interview three representatives at Janis: the CEO, who is a third-generation owner-operator of this firm; the plant manager; and the floor supervisor. This plant is 100 percent white.

The description of skills needed for the sample job lessened in complexity as I went down the hierarchy of respondents. The CEO stated that he would like operators to "have some mechanical ability as to which direction to tighten the wrench on your nut, or to loosen it. And they have to have basic math skills to do the quality-control checks that we require." This CEO said that operators performed SPC tasks and that they need to know how to add, subtract, multiply, and divide. He also noted that they need to know how to use decimals, and they "teach them the metric system, too. Now they don't convert themselves, normally our engineering department will convert it to English standards from metrics. But they have to be taught to read micrometers or calipers."

The plant manager stated that the skill he most seeks is mechanical ability,

> [t]he ones that seem to adapt for us are ones that have mechanical aptitude and that put together . . . You know, they can envision assembling or disassembling something, that have common sense. I'm not looking for a Rhodes scholar. I'm looking for someone that I can count on day in, day out. And the skill level is just that somebody that can, when the boss says, "Okay this is wrong. Make it right." And they can see their way to, "Okay, I've got to adjust this, and I've got to adjust that in order to make the part right."

He stated that it is very difficult to screen applicants for mechanical skills: "Unfortunately, it's more of a hit or miss than it is a science. . . . he can tell me that he can fix things around the house, that he works on his car day in and day out, where you would expect he's got quite an aptitude for mechanical. Set him in front of a machine, and 3 months later you're asking him to go back to where he came from, because it's not there."

The plant manager also noted that his workers tended not to have more than junior high school math or reading skills: "[M]ost of the people that we get through the front door, they don't have anything beyond your basic math. . . . it's a rare occasion when I find somebody that has had algebra, geometry, trig, that kind of high school education. It truly isn't there, so I don't have anything really to compare whether, you know . . . "

The floor supervisor stated that "basic math and reading skills—they're not really that important. They are in some cases where we have to subtract, basic stuff like that. Very little reading." He teaches workers how to use fractions and decimals: "You learn that as soon as you start coming in. It's just like starting from the beginning. . . . it's just a learning curve and that's it. . . . "

All 3 of the interviewed respondents from this firm stated that skill needs have remained stable over the past 5 years, and that the skill characteristics of applicants have not changed over this time period. However, the plant manager reported many problems with the work ethic and work attitudes among machine operators:

> I think that we run into things that amaze me. I had a gentleman that started Monday. Five and half hours into the day, went to lunch, never came back. And he was recommended by one of the gentlemen that works here. So, I think the absolute least I would do in that situation is walk up to my buddy and say "Hey, I don't know how you do this every day. I'm leaving." Not saying a word to anyone . . . People that feel no responsibility towards making sure that the customers have what they need to do, what they're trying to do. I think that the attitude is I'll work, we came in and put in our hours today and we took off . . . and we didn't want to share any of the real responsibility for what it takes to get it done.

No one interviewed at Janis reported problems with employee turnover, but it was said to have increased. The plant manager reported: "It's become just recently, but I think that that's an exception, that's definitely not a rule. The wages are high enough to retain them."

The floor supervisor, who has been with this firm for 14 years (as opposed to the plant manager's 4 years) offered an explanation for the recent deterioration of worker attitudes and higher turnover. He noted that hard skills, attitudes, and turnover of workers vary with overall market conditions:

> You know . . . when things are slow you get all kinds of people. You can get guys that are really high-skilled machinists. You get people from McDonald's. We get those kind of people. We get all types when things are slow. When things have picked up like now, and all those

other skilled people have their jobs back, you know from layoffs and things like that. You get the younger crowd, you know, 18, 19, 20 years old, and no skills.

Lionel Plastics is located 2 miles due south of Janis Snap and Tool. The firm began operations in 1950; it became a minority-owned business in 1987. The African-American CEO owns a 55 percent share of the corporation; a white-owned corporation owns the remaining 45 percent. Starting wages for a machine operator (the sample job) at Lionel are $6.70/hour, 33 percent less than at Janis. Average wages differ by 36 percent ($7.40 versus $11.50). The majority of the workers in this firm are white; 35 percent are African American.

The majority of "old timers" at this firm are white women (there is likely a wage/gender story to be told here when comparing their wages to Janis's). The white personnel manager reported that 60 percent of the new hires are men; the majority of these are African American. She felt that this change "represents the applicant pool."

Although the machine operators at Lionel work with plastic, the work they do is similar to that of the operators at Janis. At both places the machines are semiautomatic, and at both places the operator is responsible for completing quality inspections and SPC charts. There appear to be more measurement skills demanded at Janis, while Lionel workers need to have more visual observation skills because they are inspecting colored car parts that will be viewed by car owners.

The CEO of Lionel stressed that required skills are very basic: "There are some limited mathematical requirements for statistical process control that are used. It is trainable, it is basic." Workers need to be literate to "be able to read the process inspection sheet, the operator instruction sheet, to be able to read the packaging specs and know how to package products."

Lionel's head of personnel has been with the company far longer than the other respondents: 14 years. She noted that she does not feel that the applicant pool is less skilled than it was in the past (the firm has gone from white- to black-owned during this time period). The floor supervisor, like his counterpart at Janis, tended to downplay the importance of basic math; instead he accentuated the importance of observation and communication skills.

This firm has implemented new technologies and work organizational processes in the past 5 years, including more automation, SPC, and new emphasis on teamwork. The CEO stated that "because of the heightened requirements for SPC, we have gotten a little more detail in terms of training our operators. We used to do SPC more for window dressing, now we do it for the benefit that it has for our own company." However, he and the other respondents felt that these changes have not affected the type of worker they have sought over the years.

A high school degree is required for an entry-level job at Lionel so, according to the CEO, "that usually would designate a person who has gotten enough of the basic math skills and able to read at a high school to be able to do some of the things that we require." It is interesting to note that unlike the views of the plant manager and floor supervisor at Janis, Lionel's CEO felt that his workforce is more educated than it has been in the past:

> . . . the workforce that we have today, I mentioned about the work ethic, but they tend to be a little more educated, and so the training does not need to be as extensive, or as repetitive I guess would be the correct word.

Like the plant manager at Janis, the CEO at Lionel felt that there has been a deterioration in work ethic and attitude among younger workers (in fact, the variation of "what's the matter with kids these days" was commonly expressed by respondents at all firms). He noted:

> As we are getting younger people into the workforce, and we have had a number of people over the years that reach retirement age, and so you tend to hire younger people, and it appears to be (not in all of them, I do not want to stereotype them, not in all cases, but more so in terms of the norm) a decreased or diminishing work ethic.

The personnel manager, who is white, echoed his sentiments, but noted some racial differences in terms of work ethic and attitudes, saying poorer work attitudes typify " a minority" of black male employees. However, the African-American floor supervisor reported that young workers are better workers than the older group: "I don't think the older ones are really acceptable to change on the whole. . . . Yes, I have an eas-ier time with it [younger people] yeah. Now, the older ones now will work, okay? They're just not acceptable to change, as the young ones, I guess because they've been here 20 years."

In response to a complaint that a lot of people have about younger people, he stated:

Well, I haven't had a problem with it. And I guess because the job market, it's not a vast market out there, where you can really get a decent job, paying something with benefits, so some of them are willing to work. And then you have some of them that just don't want to work, you know . . . [he says these workers invariably are young]. Well, their work ethic is not like mine was. Mine was, they tell me to do a job, then boom, that was it. I would do the job. I would go to it and I would give it my best.

As reported in the previous chapter section, the floor supervisor at Lionel also noticed race differences in work ethic and attitude. Based on the perceptions of employers, it appears that these matched firms require similar skills from workers.

However, the work at Janis is considered to be "man's work," perhaps because it was once a more physically demanding process to stamp the parts and shape the bolts before the operation became automated. It is now a relatively clean and straightforward operation, done primarily by machines, with the major demand placed on workers appearing to be the ability to withstand the repetitiveness and monotony of tasks. There also is a new emphasis on observational skills, as operators have to check parts for defects after they are automatically produced.

On the supply side, the more poorly paid workers at Lionel are described as possessing similar skills to those at Janis. In fact, there were fewer complaints about hard skills among workers at Lionel than at Janis. Representatives from both organizations reported some ethic and attitude problems among younger workers. Although the African-American supervisor at Lionel reported some racial differences in work ethic and attitude, it is also clear from the comments of the plant manager at Janis that workers have such poor attitudes that they have walked away from their shift.

Respondents at Janis also reported that they are attracting workers with fewer skills than in the past (perhaps because of a tighter labor market among higher-skilled whites workers in the Detroit area, a result of increased demands in the industry). In spite of decreased hard skills and poorer attitudes among workers at Janis, there has been no adjustment down of entry-level wages.

Elizabeth Plastic Products and Mushroom Plastics

Elizabeth Plastic Products and Mushroom Plastics are well-matched firms. Mushroom Plastics, a family-owned and operated business, is located in the suburb of Warren, just one mile away from the Detroit border. Elizabeth is located about 1.5 miles northwest of Mushroom in the bordering suburb of Roseville; Elizabeth is actually about a mile farther from the northern boundary of the city of Detroit than its match.

Elizabeth began operations as a white-owned and operated firm; it was purchased by a group of whites and an African American in 1985, with the black owner holding a majority share.

Both firms produce plastic parts for the auto industry (Mushroom also produces plastic and metal parts), most often by injection molding, but also by extrusion (which uses a press and thus is a bit more physically demanding); both processes are semiautomated. The sample job for both firms is machine operator; both firms employ primarily women for these tasks (80 percent of the operators at Mushroom, and over 95 percent of the workers at Elizabeth, are women).

Although the floors at both firms appeared to be clean, well-organized and well-managed, Mushroom appears to cater to its employees more than any observed plant. The floor is decorated with plants and murals and an actual garden, surrounded by picnic tables, was planted in the center. The head of personnel reported that the firm goes out of its way to address personnel needs by holding special events and work-related recreational activities. She also stated that she will spend entire days on a machine to get a better feel for worker concerns.

There are 100 press operators at Mushroom (35 at the facility I visited, and another 65 located in a building down the street); there are also 100 press operators at Elizabeth. The workforce at Mushroom is said to be less than 5 percent black, and the president refused to provide a numerical breakdown; he also would not allow a floor supervisor to be interviewed.

Mushroom's president reported that starting pay is "the community wage, between 8 and 9 dollars"; he would neither give a more exact figure for a starting wage or any figure for the average wage. For comparative purposes, I have listed their starting wage as $8.50/hour. Elizabeth starts its workers at $5.40/hour, or 36.4 percent less than starting wages at Mushroom; 65 percent of the operators are black. Before this firm became a minority-owned business in 1984, the workforce was 95 percent white.

Mushroom Plastics demands relatively rudimentary skills of its machine operators. The most notable change the firm has implemented is a shift from individual to modular production; workers now are organized into teams and are also rotated from job to job. The head of personnel noted many disadvantages with the local workforce, stating that many applicants have not finished high school and 10 percent do not possess very basic reading and math skills. She felt the lack of basic skills is more prevalent among young people:

> I think the attitude from people is that you don't need to have any kind of education, you don't need any schooling, you just go and you run a press machine. You know, you go to a factory, your choices are when you graduate from school, if you graduate, you either go to college or you go work in a factory because factory jobs pay fairly good for not going to school. That's about all they can do, unless they want to work at McDonald's for minimum wage or some of these other places . . . it seems to run in the family or something?
>
> You wouldn't believe the number of people we have here that their mother works here and their son works here and their two daughters work here and then the daughter-in-law works here and the son-in-law works here and the cousin works here and the uncle. I mean it's incredible that they, seems like people, almost if they come from a blue-collar background, that just seems to be their niche, that's where they fit in and they pass that along and that's all they think about is working in the factory . . . [i]t's all they want to do. They don't really have the motivation or ambition, or that's their security level, that's what they want to do, don't make me do anything else, don't make me talk to people, just let me do this and that's what they feel comfortable with.

She noted that this lack of motivations puts her into a "bind," because with a new emphasis on team skills, she is requiring new skills, such as more communication and SPC:

> We're having trouble with our older workforce because they were used to running a press machine all day, not talking, not doing anything for eight hours and now all of a sudden, with having to rotate and having to be in teams and come up with ideas and suggestions and things, they're hating it.

She noted that younger workers are more open to new ideas but that they have attitude problems: "[T]hey're not as easily satisfied, they want to know why I have to do this or, you know, they pay attention to what the other workers are doing and they compare themselves and it seems like they have a lot more problems than the older worker that just wants to come in."

As noted in chapter 5, the personnel director at Mushroom relies on the services of 5 different temporary services to recruit workers, and only accepts one out of 20 for permanent employment. All workers referred from these agencies are white; the few black workers at the plant date from before this director's tenure (4 years previous to this interview).

Elizabeth Plastic Products does not have modular production per se, but the factory floor (minus the murals, plants, and picnic tables) looks remarkably similar to Mushroom's. Workers are running similar machines and are said to require similar skills. Like Mushroom, Elizabeth also now screens its applicants through the use of several temporary agencies, but they do not require a high school degree. The head of personnel for Elizabeth reported that automation has made the job of machine operator "safer and easier." The white floor manager also noted that the job is now easier in a physical sense—workers no longer have to do as much hand-trimming of parts, which often resulted in severe cuts.

Workers at Elizabeth, like those at Mushroom, are cross-trained and are required to learn SPC, although they do not perform it on as regular a basis as Mushroom's operators. The head of personnel noted:

> . . . individuals cannot inspect every single part that we make, especially when you talk about the number of parts that we make, so each individual has a touch of that, a taste of that. And what typically happens is, when someone goes on any type of disability as well as vacation, someone else slides into that spot. Well, that's when they start getting that. So if Janie goes on vacation, she's on SPC and she has another person down there that has an interest in going into SPC, what she would do is make sure a supervisor knows I'm interested in that position and what he would do is when that person goes on vacation, so and so is going on vacation this week, would you please handle SPC. For about 2 or 3 days he'll do some training with them so he can take over. And that's how we fill the slots, sometimes the slots are filled by another shift, first or third shift someone saying, look, but there's also somebody on the shift that you're constantly trying to train to step into that slot.

Unfortunately, because of taping problems, there are no transcriptions of the head of personnel's perceptions of employee work ethic and attitude.[14]

The floor supervisor oversees 17 first-shift workers who, because of seniority, are primarily white (all but a few of these workers date from the time that the firm was solely white-owned. The first shift is the most desirable of the three shifts the plant currently runs).

The floor manager at Elizabeth appeared to be unhappy about the change in ownership and the resultant change in worker composition. He said that morale among his workers was low and attitudes are poor:

> Being on the day shift, I have the most senior people, which have made it this far because their attendance is fair and their ability and their work is good. I don't really have a big problem with attendance. What happens with the older people is their attitude kicks in . . . they see new operators come in from the second or third shift, making almost as much as they have, and they've been here 10 years. [He also noted the average wage among these long-time workers is $6/hour.]

The floor manager noted his own role changed and that he did not interact with his staff the way he once did because of downsizing: "[W]hat I am is a glorified machine adjuster. I don't get the time to supervise people." It also appears that the changing racial composition of the firm is affecting workers on his shift (nearly all are white). The floor supervisor noted that: "[T]he way things used to run, peoplewise, is not the same. In the old days the shift was one big family . . . " He later stated:

> . . . that to raise the number of black workers you have to counteract the older people on my shift, which are mostly white . . . that upsets some people because they see all that this company is hiring in new people are black. I've heard comments. I don't know if it upsets the way things are run, but I think it is making people unhappy.

This match is one where it appears that there are some differences in skill demands—Mushroom Plastics is now demanding that all workers complete SPC tasks on a regular basis, and that workers contribute more to their teams in terms of input and responsibility.

However, workers there are said to have not yet mastered communication and teamwork skills and that interviewed representatives from other firms and training programs stressed that the performance of SPC requires little more than the ability to count and use a calculator. It therefore appears unlikely that the relatively recent institution of these task changes provides the rationale for the wage difference between the two firms.

One the other hand, the institution of greater skill demands at Mushroom, coupled with the change at Elizabeth from a largely white to now largely black workforce, may be factors that have entrenched preexisting wage differences and assured their continuation into the future.

Summary: Three High-paying Firms and Their Low-paying Matches

Although just under half of all respondents perceived skill differences between black and white workers, it is unclear, when looking at high-paying white-owned firms and their black-owned matches, that such skill differences can account for the magnitude of the wage differences presented here.

There is a 35 percent wage difference between white-owned Lackawanna and black-owned Cannon Chemical. However, skill requirements are described to be slightly higher at Cannon, and in contrast to the situation at Lackawanna, where the plant manager reported problems with both the hard and soft skills of workers, there were few complaints about either hard or soft skills at the black-owned firm. In fact, the respondent at Cannon had indicated that he was able to hire individuals with some college for entry-level jobs there. From the evidence presented here, it appears that history and tradition (the plant manager reported that they have started workers at $10/hour for 10 years), has more to do with the high wages paid at Lackawanna than the demands of the job or the characteristics of the workforce.

There is a 36 percent difference in starting wages between white-owned Janis Snap and Tool and Lionel Plastics, its black-owned match. Both of these firms have made technological and organizational changes. Although Janis makes metal parts, and Lionel makes plastic parts, production processes at both firms are highly automated, and workers primarily take produced parts off the machine and inspect them. There were complaints about workers' attitudes and ethics at both firms, although there were more complaints about hard skill deficiencies at Janis.

In all, it appears that the high wages paid at Janis may be better explained by gender more than skills. The workforce there is entirely male, a holdover from the time before automation when metal parts production was a dirty process that required physical strength. In contrast, the workforce at Lionel is primarily female, dating from the time when the workforce did more plastic assembly work than parts production (fine assembly in the auto-supply industry has been traditionally undertaken by women).

Finally, the 35 percent starting wage difference at white-owned Mushroom and Elizabeth Plastic Products, its black-owned match, may be partly explained by differences in skill requirements. Performance of SPC tasks are part of the job description at Mushroom, while such tasks are only required of Elizabeth workers on a sporadic basis. On the other hand, there were more complaints about hard skills at Mushroom, where long-time white workers, described as friends and relatives of each other, were said to be especially lacking in the hard skills necessary to do the job. It does not seem that existing worker characteristics are related to the higher wages paid there, though there may be the hope that higher start-ing wages will attract new workers with more skills. The CEO's empha-sis of the fact that they pay the "community" wage may also reflect a different supply and demand situation in the suburbs than that which ex-ists in the city.

CONCLUSION: RACE, LOCATION, AND SKILLS

There is clearly a skills story told here that cannot be ignored. Nearly three-fourths of respondents indicated that there are either racially or ge-ographically determined skill differences among workers. Just under half of both white and black employers indicated that there are racial differ-ences in skills. Most discussed skill differences were in math and read-ing; employers were most likely to attribute these differences to geographically determined differences in educational resources rather than race per se.

Many employers also discussed some "neighborhood effects" of liv-ing in the city, including poor schools, a lack of role models, and a sense of hopelessness and defeat that they felt translated into skill differences between black and white workers. In addition, most employers who dis-cussed these negative impacts of city residence noted that they also af-fected city whites.

However, the effect of the explanation of a skills mismatch between urban blacks and the skill demands of available jobs here is somewhat analogous to findings relating to the effects of spatial mismatch pre-sented in chapter 5. In chapter 5, I noted that geographical distance and poor transportation options are factors that clearly exist, but given the ev-idence of firms located far from the boundaries of the city of Detroit that have hired African Americans in significant numbers, distance in itself can only partially explain the failure of young, urban African-American workers to pursue suburban job opportunities.

Similarly, differences in job skill requirements and/or described racially or locationally based worker skill differences, although apparently evident, seem to contribute only partially to the stark wage discrepancies shown among firms with largely white workforces compared to those that are majority black. This is because stated skill differences do not appear profound; it does not seem from the statements provided by employers, and from my observations of workers at work, that they can account for the magnitude of the noted wage differences between workers in firms with either largely white or majority-black workforces. The tasks involved in both the described low- and higher-paying entry-level jobs, as well as the attributes of very low-paid and relatively high-paid workers, appear to be too similar to explain these wage gaps.

There is a caveat to the evidence presented here: employer interviews allow a more detailed measurement of required skills than, for example, the stated years of education required for a job used in more quantitative analyses; yet it is still difficult to gauge either the range and depth of skills required for jobs, or the skill-related characteristics of the workforce, from an interview lasting an average of 90 minutes or from a cursory view of workers at work.

However, there are interesting findings here that could pave the way for more research. Specifically, it is interesting to note that the "soft" skill deficits among African Americans reported by other authors, by Wilson (1996) in particular, do not seem to carry much weight in this sample. The responses of my employers may be different than Wilson's because only 5 of the 26 firms in my sample had a workforce that was less than 35 percent black, while 61 percent had majority-black workforces. As noted, fully 57 percent of Wilson's respondents stated that they had no contact with black workers, and he does not report the racial composition of his studied firms.

It is also interesting to note that 4 employers who hired both white and black workers from the city of Detroit stated here that work attitude and effort is actually perceived to be better among urban blacks than among urban whites.

In addition, it does appear that factors apart from the human capital characteristics of workers, or the skill demands of jobs, could be said to contribute to wage discrepancies shown here. Actual instances and the remnants of "crowding," where the concentration of certain groups, such as African Americans or women, into relatively low-paying jobs drives down wages and wage premiums to favored groups, can be seen playing out among these studied firms in terms of both race and gender.

Note the higher wage paid to the all-male workforce at Janis, where "valorous" work once was, but no longer is, physically demanding. In addition, the low wages paid at the now black-owned Elizabeth Plastic Products, and Lionel, were once paid to a majority-white female workforce. Even though these jobs are attracting both black men and women, the wages remain low compared to the all-male or all-white workforces of Janis or Mushroom Plastics.

Perhaps the comparison of Cannon and Lackawanna is the most stark example of wage-setting that defies human capital (or "quality sorting") explanations for wage discrepancies in firms. In the case of Cannon Chemical, far lower wages were paid to an all-black workforce that was described as having *better* skills and attitudes than its much higher-paying all-white match.

Clearly, this information provides a caution for conclusions drawn from studies broadly looking at the effect of test scores, educational attainment, or even employer-based statements of changing skill needs, on wages. More research within occupational categories at the firm level—research including more actual observation of workers at work than I was able to complete here—is needed for a better understanding of how employer skill needs, and worker characteristics, most likely in interaction with other factors, may affect the relative economic standing of urban minorities.

NOTES

[1]Firm pairs were *not* initially matched by skill needs and job tasks. Once an interview was conducted at a black-owned firm, a sample job was identified. The white respondent was told about the characteristics of this job as if such a job description were sought for all interviewed firms, and was asked to focus on a job with similar tasks as the "sample job."

[2]This is the "quality sorting" explanation for why predominantly black industries and occupations pay lower wages than predominantly white industries and occupations. See Hirsch and Macpherson (1993) for a recent discussion of this model, and Baron and Newman (1990) for a critique of it. The latter authors contend that "jobs" offer a more precise measure of labor market segmentation than broad categories of occupations across firms and industries.

[3]Just because worker skills and work requirements may be described similarly does not mean that they are indeed similar. As indicated later in this chapter, a longer-term direct observation of workers at work is necessary to make a judgment of similarity or difference. Employer views are presented in the context of this caveat.

[4]In addition, the head of operations at Curve-All reported that he thought skill needs had increased, but he could not say how. When viewing the workers, it was impossible to see how the sort of work they performed required any skills other than endurance (they fed metal into presses and did not perform any quality checks—these were done by others). Therefore, I did not include him in this group.

[5]The floor supervisor at Satellite Fasteners, for example, said that customer demands for quality have dictated his stated change in required skills.

[6]Conversation with Richard Murnane, October 1995.

[7]These firms are Mushroom Plastics, Satellite Fasteners, Maybee Inc., Morgan Stamping (whose CEO says she actually prefers a GED, which she feels provides greater assurance that the applicant is literate), and Sears Metals; all but Mushroom are black-owned.

[8]I did not gather the opinions of 7 respondents. This is not a reflection of these respondents' refusal to address the topic. Not a single respondent refused outright to address racial questions, other than the two respondents at Sergeant Gum—who, on ostensibly moral grounds, would only speak in terms of location. The other respondents either felt that they could not address racial or locational issues because they had workers from only one category (i.e., all white or all black, or all city: this is especially true about locational issues). One respondent's comments were omitted because of poor tape quality; another because time constraints did not allow us to get to the race questions that I asked at the end of the interview. A complete breakdown of respondents' responses in regard to racial and locational effects on perceived skills is included in Appendix B.

[9]A number of respondents, when they saw racial skill differences among workers, were apt to say that the differences were true only for black men and not for black women (see Appendix C). Kirschenman and Neckerman (1991b) discussed the fact that white employers perceived skill differences between black men and women, and were apt to prefer hiring black women if they hired blacks at all. I did not pursue these stated gender differences in my study because there did not seem to be enough incidents of perceived "gender within race" differences here to study in any organized manner. However, the reported observations here, along with more pervasive evidence from other studies (including MCSUI findings—where I was more apt to hear about differences between black men and women from primarily white respondents), points to a rich area in which to pursue further research.

[10]Locational skill differences are also delineated in Appendix B.

[11]These scholars note that this trend is especially true among lower-level white-collar employees who are now expected to perform a wider variety of tasks for lower wages. Two examples from this study of wages reduced for reasons

other than skill-based reasons are Armstrong Industries, which is now paying almost half of what such workers were paid 6 years ago, with no changes in skill requirements; and Dartmouth Stamping, where workers have not only recently taken a relatively small hourly pay cut when work demands are increasing but are also paid 60 percent less than workers performing exactly the same jobs at another facility owned by their parent corporation.

[12]I selected these firms on the basis of wages; I chose the firms with the highest starting wages to obtain the biggest "gap" among their matches. See Appendix C for a listing of sample jobs, their stated requirements, and worker skill characteristics.

[13]Poor verbal communication and comprehension skills among blacks have been described in previous studies (e.g., Moss and Tilly, 1991b) as well as by some MCSUI respondents (note descriptions of workers at Hammers Department Store, Livonia, in chapter 5), as well as by respondents in this study—as reported later on in this chapter.

[14]This interview was held in a cubicle directly adjacent to the factory floor; half of it was wiped out by background noise.

CHAPTER 7

The Persistence of Discrimination and Policy Recommendations

The findings of this study, including the low wages paid to urban blacks "crowded" in firms willing to hire them, what appears to be discriminatory hiring practices of largely white suburban firms, the harassment of black workers in the suburbs, and the higher percentages of black workers in firms with black owners and/or strictly enforced affirmative action policies, all point to the fact that racial discrimination persists in metropolitan Detroit, and that it may be a factor in the wage discrepancies reported found among these studied firms.

These findings, based on the outcome of a qualitative study in a relatively small sample, are neither definitive nor generalizable, but they must be addressed in the context of a literature that posits that discriminatory treatment in the labor market is a major cause of earnings and employment inequality between blacks and whites. The evidence in this literature is broad and includes results of audit studies, correspondence studies, careful wage and employment regression studies, and reported discrimination suits (Darity and Mason, 1998).[1]

However, as both the literature on the subject and the findings from this study emphasize, the manifestation and the effects of discrimination are not simple; the labor-force problems of urban blacks are complex and self-reinforcing.

For example, with regard to spatial factors, employers interviewed as part of this and the MCSUI study confirm earlier research, which demonstrates that spatial issues are very important in both work search behavior and employment probabilities. It is extremely difficult for urban residents without cars to search for higher-paying jobs adequately along the Groesbeck Corridor; searches are made even more difficult by employers whose sole means of recruitment are signs in their windows, or word of mouth among their workers. Yet spatial barriers can at least be partially overcome by more equitable and inclusive hiring procedures. The issues of hiring practices and space interact.

In addition, the out-migration of jobs from the city to outlying sub-urbs, and now from border suburbs to ex-urban areas, can be seen as a contributing factor to the wage discrepancies that we see in this study. Increased competition from black urban residents for a shrinking number of geographically accessible jobs may be driving wages down among employers willing to hire larger percentages of black workers. Wage and space issues interact.

Spatial barriers to higher-paying jobs also impede access to better means of transportation (a car is unaffordable to a minimum-wage worker), and also lessen the probability that workers will have the funds to move from the city to areas with better school districts. Space and job search factors interact.

Similarly, in regard to skill-based explanations for wage discrepancies: the majority of employers in this sample perceive differences in skills between black and white workers and/or city and suburban workers regardless of race. These racial and geographically determined differences point to the larger institutional issues that sustain "spatial mismatches": that the pattern of nearly all-white suburbs surrounding a largely black central city has clear implications for the quality of education and other services that can be offered to the residents of Detroit. Thus, space and skill issues are intertwined.

Even though racial, spatial, and skill-based factors all appear to contribute to the wage and employment disparities between white and blacks seen here, some explanatory factors appear to exert more influence than others. For example, higher-paying, white-owned suburban firms had far lower percentages of black workers than either black-owned firms or white-owned firms that had either elected or were compelled to use strong affirmative action hiring policies. These findings, when viewed along with those from hiring audit studies, and the findings of Moss and Tilly (1991b) that firms often move to follow targeted white workforces, undermine the simple notion of "spatial mismatch."

Institutional discriminatory attitudes and practices created the spatial mismatch we see between the city of Detroit and its suburbs. Thus, "spatial mismatch," while partly due to purely economic factors relating to finding cheaper land for housing and new production processes, also results from persistent racial animosities and discrimination that find their expression through spatial variables.

Therefore, purely space-based policies, such as improving transportation options for city workers, to ameliorate the problem of economic disparities between largely white suburban and largely black urban populations can be helpful (Holzer and Ihlanfeldt, 1995). However, they cannot in themselves adequately address the larger institutional practices that continue to sustain separate societies of blacks and whites in the Detroit metropolitan area and in other metropolitan areas throughout the country.

It was interesting to note that interviewed Detroit employers, who seemed to understand the lives of their urban black workers and were sympathetic to their needs, may not have read William Julius Wilson, but were very cognizant of issues of "neighborhood effects" such as poor schools, a lack role models, and the simple psychological stress of living in a deteriorated, impoverished area on job performance and employment outcomes. In fact, Cutler and Glaeser (1995) address the issue of spatial mismatch by identifying what they call its "weak form"; they contend that racial residential segregation harms all black residents of a metropolitan area, whether or not these residents live in a segregated area (cited in Moss and Tilly, 1998).

Therefore, the policy recommendations needed to address the effects of spatial mismatch must also address its root causes: persistent employment and housing discrimination. In addition, policies must also acknowledge how space and skill issues interact to effect the economic outcomes of urban blacks, such as better schooling, on-the-job training and mentoring in both "hard" and "soft" skills.

EXISTING ANTIDISCRIMINATION POLICY AND ITS LIMITATIONS

Of primary policy importance is the need to overcome the negative attitudes of employers toward black applicants and workers through stronger and better enforced antidiscrimination measures in hiring. If such measures were in place it would be easier to overcome skill, space, and other wage-related aspects of the employment problems of urban blacks. It is clear from the case studies presented here that antidiscrimination and affirmative action programs implemented at the firm level have proven to be successful in certain organizations in the Detroit metropolitan area in increasing the number of black workers; it is also clear that when such policies are implemented within the context of a strong union or a public-sector setting, wages do not fall with an increase of black workers.

Currently, two federal vehicles address hiring discrimination. The first is widely targeted sanctions (which affect the decisions of all employers in a labor or product market simultaneously), and the other is selective sanctions, which affect decisions of those employers with direct contact with enforcement agencies. Widely targeted sanctions are ordered and enforced through Executive Order No. 11246 as amended by Executive Order No. 11275 and administered by the Office of Federal Contract Compliance Programs (OFCCP). These orders impose a basic obligation on federal contractors not to discriminate and require them to use affirmative action in order to employ minorities and women, and to get similar commitments from their subcontractors. Widely targeted sanctions affect all employers who bid on federal construction contracts. Sanctions include back pay orders, retroactive seniority requirements, cancellation or suspension of existing bids, and exclusion from bids on future government contracts.

The vehicle for selective sanctions is Title VII of the Civil Rights Act, which allows individuals to sue employers for discrimination. This act also gives authority to the Equal Employment Opportunity Commission (EEOC) to impose sanctions on discrimination by private employers and federal government agencies in administrative or judicial proceedings (Mincy, 1991).

Historically, the EEOC used this authority to establish broad legal principles, which sometimes resulted in multimillion dollar judgments against discriminating employers (Leonard, 1990; Darity and Mason, 1998). Title VII also allows the Justice Department to bring suits against state and local government units charged with employment discrimination.

Public agencies responsible for enforcing antidiscrimination laws receive a large flow of complaints annually. In 1988 alone (the latest year for which detailed data have been released), 50,477 charges of discrimination in employment on the basis of race, ethnicity, or national origin were filed with the federal Equal Opportunity Commission and its state and local counterparts. However, since the early 1980s, enforcement activities of the EEOC have stagnated under a combination of inadequate resources and leadership ambivalent about the agency's mission (Bendick, 1993).

During these years, conservatives charged that American economic productivity and competitiveness were undermined through the chronic overuse of antiemployment discrimination litigation (Olson, 1992). At the same time, 5 supreme court rulings substantially reduced the power and scope of antidiscrimination laws. In the 1980s heads of federal agencies challenged the use of timetables and numerical goals in the affirmative action plans of federal contractors and of affirmative action hiring plans in judgments and conciliation agreements involving state and local government bodies found guilty of past discrimination (Mincy, 1991). The passage of the Civil Rights Act of 1991, which reversed some Supreme Court rulings, occurred after a prolonged and bitter debate.

The limitations of current legislation abound. Leonard (1990), showed that federal contractor antidiscrimination programs had only modest effects on black employment (Mincy, 1991). For example, the affirmative action requirements for government contractors have little potential to reduce employment discrimination in the retail trade and service sectors, which have few federal contractors (Smith and Welch, 1984), yet 85 percent of the audited applicants who received unfavorable treatment were seeking jobs in these industries. Mincy also stresses that, given the results of auditing studies, an emphasis on government contractors (although this legislation has positively influenced the hiring of blacks in Big Three firms), is not sufficient in today's labor market.

AN AUDIT METHODOLOGY TO
ADDRESS HIRING DISCRIMINATION

Harry Holzer emphasizes policies to target the demand side of the labor market through the passage of strengthened Equal Opportunity legislation and Affirmative Action programs. He notes, however, that employer reliance on particular recruitment and screening strategies reduces the pool of black applicants and lessens the chance that there will be black applicants to file complaints (1996).

One small step that can be taken to reduce hiring discrimination is used effectively to reduce discrimination in housing: the use of paired auditors to target and legally sanction discriminating employers.

As can be seen by the evidence presented here and in other studies, many firms (especially smaller ones and/or nonfederal contractors) rely heavily on referrals from current employees and on recruiting that is targeted toward white neighborhoods (Kirschenman and Neckerman, 1991; Holzer, 1995).

Increased use of paired black and white auditors, while expensive, could deal with this problem. Testers can participate in litigation either as plaintiffs or as witnesses corroborating allegations of discrimination by actual job seekers (Bendick, 1993).

The use of auditors to enhance the effectiveness of current antidiscrimination legislation appears to be particularly pressing at this point in time in which the political tide is moving against the practices and principles of affirmative action, and when politicians and the popular press have promoted the notion that not only has existing antidiscrimination legislation been so successful that we don't need it anymore, but that indeed, whites are suffering from the effects of reverse discrimination.

Minimally, the use of hiring audit studies can do much to raise the American consciousness about the persistence of racism, as well as proving discrimination claims and enforcing antidiscrimination sanctions.

SKILLS

Although employment discrimination should be directly addressed through the legal mechanisms that still survive, there is still a need to address the ramifications of discrimination that has existed now for generations. As Darity and Mason (1998) stress, changes in social as well as legal institutions are needed to address its persistent effects.

City schools just do not have the resources and programs that suburban schools do. They are often severely underfunded and graduate poorly educated students, some of whom, as Orfield (1992) has pointed out in his study of Chicago schools, return to inner-city schools to teach. As long as white residents and businesses continue to leave cities and housing discrimination persists in the suburbs, the skills of blacks who graduate from central-city schools will be inferior to those of whites with similar years of education.

Thus, more equitable plans for school funding are warranted. In Michigan, over 25 years ago, the Supreme Court case of *Bradley v. Milliken,* which proposed the metropolitanization of school districts, was rejected. Although such legislation seems particularly unfeasible in this time of charter schools and growing private school enrollment, other policies to equalize resources among school districts, such as those enacted at the state or federal level, are needed.

However, Orfield (1992) stressed that the onus for improving the marketable skills of black youth should not fall solely on schools. Barring changes in schools, subsidizing industry to provide pertinent training to black youth is an alternative for raising their skills.

Policies ought to be considered that help black adolescents gain a clear understanding of the demands of actual jobs through their apprenticeship in actual workplaces; preferably ones that have black role models in management positions, and stress the acquisition both hard and soft skills. Higher-earning occupations often stress math and science skills, as well as abilities related to flexibility, teamwork, and decision-making. A noteworthy change among blacks and whites is that fewer black male college graduates are represented in management than they were in the 1970s. Holzer (1995) writes that:

> . . . approaches to raising information and contact with adults and employers for young blacks, such as mentoring programs and various employer-school linkages, should also be explored. Proposals for youth apprenticeships which are currently popular among some might be particularly effective ways of improving access, skills, and long-run wages all at once (p. 30).

It is possible that public funds now reserved for vocational education could be used for these purposes. Federal educational funds could also be earmarked for participating firms, and tax incentives might also be used.

In addition, Murnane (1992) observes:

> Changing the skills students learn in school so as to make graduates more capable of working productively in workplaces in which teamwork and initiative are valued, will require transforming schools into organizations where these behavioral patterns are also paramount.

Schools, then, need the same type of overhaul that "best practice" firms have accomplished. Therefore, industry links stressing an interplay of school and work, as well as on-the-job training in such skills as filling out applications, interviewing, and appropriate on-the-job behaviors, would be helpful.

EDUCATING EMPLOYERS

Finally, as Newman and Stack (1992) stress, there is a clear need to educate employers. The hiring audit studies demonstrate that employers react to black job candidates differently. The employers in this study who recognized cultural differences and increased monetary rewards for well-performed work had less turnover and fewer complaints than employers who did not engage in such practices. Again, a notion of creating either direct subsidies or tax incentives to employers who train workers and train themselves (perhaps in reeducation camps or retreats) to encourage a more racially diverse workforce may be a worthwhile approach.

NOTES

[1]*The Journal of Economic Perspectives,* volume 12, No. 2, Spring 1998 contains several excellent articles about the persistence of discrimination in both the labor and housing markets. The Darity and Mason article is included in this collection.

APPENDIX A

Sample Job Wages and Benefits
Table A-1. Sample Job Wages and Benefits

Black Firm	Samp. Job % Black	Start. Wage	Ave. Wage	Max. Wage	Benefits	White Firm	Samp. Job % Black	Start. Wage	Av. Wage	Max. Wage	Benefits
City Firms											
Cannon	97%	$6.50	$8	$12	Vac 1-3 wk Sick days Prof Share Bonus	**Lackawanna**	0%	$10	$13.00	$15	Vac 1-4 wk 5 sick days, Hlth, dnt, op 401k Ed reimb
Curve-All	100%	$4.50	$4.50	un-known	Vac Hlth	**Maybee**	80%	$7.64	$12.00	un-known	Vac 1-3 wk Hlth, dnt, op Life ins Pension
Crowe	50%	$8.50	$8.50	un-known	Vac 2 wk Hlth, dnt, op	**TopPoint**		$5.00		$7.64	Vac 1-3 wk Hlth
Trail	100%	$4.50	$5.50	$6	Vac Hosp	**FlameBest**	40%	$7	$7.50		None
Sears	90%	$4.75	$5.25	$6	Vac 1-2 wk 5 sick Hlth, op	**Gratiot**	9%	$5.50	$6.50	un-known	None

Table A-1. Sample Job Wages and Benefits (*cont.*)

Black Firm	Samp. Job % Bl	Start. Wage	Ave. Wage	Max. Wage	Benefits	White Firm	Samp. Job % Bl	Start Wage	Av. Wage	Max. Wage	Benefits
Satellite	30%	$7	$7.50	$12.50	Vac Sick Hlth, dnt Life ins Ed reimb	Planet	50%	$7.25-8.70	$8.70		Vac 1+ Pd holiday Hlth, dnt Drug rehab Life ins Ed reimb Prof share
Morgan	87%	$5.50	$6.00	$7	Vac 2 wk Hlth Ed reimb	Dartmouth	35%	$5.85	$7.00		Hlth, dnt, op 7 Sick (unp) Pd holiday Retirement
Silver	72%	$5	$5.50	$6	Vac Unpd holiday	Sargeant	50%	$6.50	$7.00	$10	Prof share
CalOran	100%	$6.50	$8	$10	Vac 1 wk Hlth, dnt Short disab 401k Ed reimb	Armstrong	50%	$7.73	$10.20	$13.37	Hlth, dnt Life ins

Firm	%	Wages	Union	Benefits
Wooward		No info.		Vac 2-3 wk; Hlth, dnt; Short disab
Amerigas		$11 $13		Ed reimb
Mushroom	5%	$8.50 won't tell un-known		Vac, Hlth; None
Janis	0%	$10 $11.50 $14.50	UAW	Vac 1+; Hlth, dnt; Sick; Life ins; Ed reimb
Mash	3%	$7.15 $10.20		Vac 1-4 wk; Pers days; Death, jury; Hlth, dnt, op; Vac 1-2 wk; Sick, holiday; Ed reimb

Suburban Firms

Firm	%	Wages
USG	0%	$11.00 $13.00
Elizabeth	65%	$5.45 $6.10 $8
Lionel	35%	$6.70 $7.40 $8.10
Twain	88%	$5.71 $6.33 $7.36

APPENDIX B

Perceived Skill Differences Between Black and White and City and Suburban Workers

Table B-1. Perceived Skill Differences

Firm	Respondent	Racial Differences?	Locational Differences?	Gen. Comments Race/Gender
Cannon Chem.	D. Glenn: CEO Nyab Muam: Supervisor	**Yes** N/A: poor record	**Yes** Black/white differences same thing as city/suburb	
Curve-All	T. Ransom: Head of Operations W. Indigo: Supervisor	**Yes** N/A: 100% black workforce	N/A—does not know city whites N/A	WI does not see race diff. but does see gender diff.
Crowe Products	P. Manning: President Jim Schmidt: Supervisor	**No:** no diff. in educational attainment **Yes:** whites "pick up quicker"—no racial diff. in soft skills	No Yes	All blacks fr. city All whites fr. sub.
Trail Industries	Sylvia Pratt: VP Howard Pratt Oper. Man.	No No	No No	

Sears Metals			
Debra Louis: President Bob Cantwell: Part-owner and Supervisor	**Yes:** education, not ability—no diff. in soft skills. **No:** but black work ethic better. Black men more nervous when interviewing; feels young whites have worse attitudes.	N/A—did not address **No**	BC notes black skills better than in past
Satellite Fasteners			
Bill Loman: Owner	**Yes:** but differences minor—whites have more mechanical skills	did not address	Both think black women more job-oriented, more pushed by families to excel—no gender diff. in soft skills. VW thinks black women are better workers than white men
Virgil Wolfe: Supervisor	**Yes:** blacks have poorer verbal skills; less job experience—have been looking for work more	**Yes:** in terms of work experience	
Silver			
Ron Silver: CEO	**No:** all in "same economic boat." "May talk diff.—but that's it." Blacks more motivated.	**Yes:** test failures higher among city residents	Black women more dependable
Denise Waring: Personnel Dir.	**No:** overall, except blacks not as effective at interviewing or filling out applications.	**No** (for job): Detroit workers have more skills than 5 years ago but more spotty work records.	DW also notes that blacks are more educated than in recent past. Black women better workers.
Fred Renning: Supervisor	Black outperform whites on floor. **No:** except he can't find blacks with set-up skills.		Black men esp. fearful during interviews. Black women more dependable

Table B-1. Perceived Skill Differences (*cont.*)

Firm	Respondent	Racial Differences?	Locational Differences?	Gen. Comments Race/Gender
Woodward Gas	Mick Findott: Owner/CEO	**Yes**	**Yes:** but Detroit whites and blacks the same	Thinks black women workers better than black men.
CalOrange	Greg Thinge: Oper. Mngr.	Did not add	Did not add	(time limits)
	Helen Haley: Personnel Dir.	**No:** But blacks more likely to have graduated high school and have spottier work histories	Did not add	HH thinks black women better workers "don't bring as much baggage" to workplace. Women have better interviewing skills—more relaxed.
Elizabeth Plastic Products	Micky Taylor: Personnel Dir.	**No:** whites a bit more likely to pass tests and tend to be drop-outs while blacks are HS grads **Yes:** soft skills	**No:** no difference betw. city and suburb. skill levels	60% applicants fail drug test—equally true for blacks and whites
	Ron Betz: Supervisor		**Yes:** city workers have worse attitudes	

Lionel			
Carl Johnson: CEO	No: only difference betw. older and younger		Does not see gender differences
Marie Scrimo: Personnel Dir.	Yes: blacks have more sporadic work histories—more likely to have been temp workers. Black and white abilities re applications: "equally bad." Blacks have poorer interviewing skills.	Yes: suburbanites calmer—less friction (both black and white)	Black applicants better educated than in past
Sol Bird: Supervisor	Yes: attitude problems more prevalent among young black males	Yes: Does not hire city whites. Thinks suburban whites have poor attitudes—walk off job.	SB says black men more likely to have poor interviewing skills—yet states it is small proportion of black men with these problems. Black women have better work ethic than black men.
Twain Plastics			
Jim Twain: CEO	Yes	No: city whites and whites from poor suburbs comparable to city blacks	
Tom Coles: Supervisor	No	Yes: notes suburban blacks have better skills than city blacks	
Lackawanna			
Ken Vetter: President	Yes: economic issue	Yes: Detroit wker inferior regardless of race	
Dan Mulvay: Personnel Dir.	No	Did not add.	
Dave Devarti: Plant Mngr.	No: but applications different	No: downriver workers have same poor skills	

Table B-1. Perceived Skill Differences (*cont.*)

Firm	Respondent	Racial Differences?	Locational Differences?	Gen. Comments Race/Gender
Maybee	Lester Maybee: Head of Oper. Jerry Rivers: Supervisor	**No:** all depends on how you structure work—not skills of workers No	**No:** (both) LM: suburbanites as difficult to retrain— whole workforce poorly educated	Workers defeated; area creates sense of hopelessness
TopPoint Prod.	Mike Rourke: Plant Manager	**No:** feels black workers are more sensitive to criticism	**N/A:** no suburban workers	Everyone from Detroit (white and black). Black women have less absenteeism than black men.
Flamebest	Paul Paris: Co-owner/supervisor	No	**Yes:** city workers have more family problems	Feels that skill differences are apparent among those who attend public and parochial schools.
Gratiot Welding	Jim Gratiot: Owner/supervisor	**Yes:** city people have more difficulty with writing and presentation skills	**Yes:** whole difference civilization in Detroit— but Detroit whites and blacks same	Feels applicant pool is more skilled than in the past

Dartmouth			
Jim Marrow: CEO	**Yes:** blacks have poorer communication skills, but training a "nightmare" for both whites and blacks	**No:** workers from city intelligent but poorly educated	Workforce has more skills than in the past. Both think poor skills of workers reflect low wages they pay. JM: "women more dependable, resign themselves to what they can get." TL thinks black women good workers but harder to deal with—both black and white women better workers—a gender thing.
Tim Looney: Supervisor	**Yes:** blacks come in with fewer skills, but no difference in ability once they are there—later states that blacks are better learners than whites	**Yes:** but suburban whites "uneducated as well"—thinks city whites same as city blacks	
Sargeant Gum			
Jim Morris: CEO	**No:** says he sees no skill differences between black and white	**Yes:** city workers do more poorly on skill tests but both city and suburban workers bad 15 years ago and they're bad today	DS feels black women are more work-oriented than black men
Dan Stack: Personnel Dir.	**No:** Blacks and whites score similarly on "reliability test"	**Yes:** also notes that suburban workers have poor skills	
Armstrong Industries	William Romeo: Personnel Director	**No:** Blacks "good productive" workers, but sometimes have transportation prob. No diff. in interviewing skills	**No**	WR sees differences in work ethic between black men and women—sees this as a "maturity" and not a race issue
	Felix Mendell: Prod. Mngr.	**No:** Same amount of problems with each group.	**Yes:** suburbanites more likely to try to advance. Suburbanites more likely to flunk drug tests.	

Table B-1. Perceived Skill Differences (*cont.*)

Firm	Respondent	Racial Differences?	Locational Differences?	Gen. Comments Race/Gender
USG	W. Herland: Manager	No	No	
Mushroom	B. Johnstone: CEO G. Toles: Personnel Director	N/A—not enough blacks Yes: soft skills only (black workers have poorer attitudes)— also noted whites are unmotivated	N/A No: lots of problems with local workforce— white illiterates and high school dropouts	GT goes through 20 temps for one hire
Janis Snap	L. Metzger: CEO Jim Hesse: Plant Mngr. Tim Tielman: Supervisor	N/A—No blacks Very surprised at discrimination in firm—no black workers. Did not address	Did not address	Whites have problems with work ethic, communication, and hard skills
Mash Inc.	George Zarycky: CEO	Yes: among applicants, not among workers. Sees differences in writing, not verbal, skills	Did not address	Feels white workers lack reasoning and hard skills—go through 10 workers before he finds a "keeper"

Sample Job and Worker Skill Characteristics
Table C-1. Sample Job and Worker Skill Characteristics

Bl. Firm/% Black	Samp. Job	Req. Skills	Worker Char.	Wh. Firm/% Black	Samp. Job	Req. Skills	Worker Char.
Cann. Chem. 97%	Paint Prod.	Wkers. mix paint—"like cooking"—use recipes/measurement. 10th-grade math and reading—no changes in req. skills	Skill levels impr. but hard to find in pool—no reported skill problems among those hired	**Lack. Chem 0%**	Paint Prod.	Job req. "few" skills. Most valued skill is "to imagine" colors: wkers need to be literate—know basic fractions.	Wkers have problems with written and verbal communication skills. There was some tension over late pay increase.
Curve-All 100%	Press Oper.	Wkers hand-feed press machines: need few skills. Described as "oily" repetitious work. Do quality inspection: SPC.	Wkers have "social problems," drugs and alcohol. Poor attitude and high turnover.	**Maybee 80%**	Entry Prod.	Range of activities from janitorial to quality checks of forged parts. Use micrometer, SPC. Will be trained to do forging. Have illiterate trainees.	All training OTJ. Workforce is poorly educated, has poor attitudes (black and white). But bad attitudes noted among managers (fired 18 managers recently).

Table C-1. Sample Job and Worker Skill Characteristics (*cont.*)

Bl. Firm/% Black	Samp. Job	Req. Skills	Worker Char.	Wh. Firm/% Black	Samp. Job	Req. Skills	Worker Char.
Crowe Prod. 50%	Prod. Wker	Weighs steel product and wraps it for shipping. Skill needs incr. Need to be able to read and write—fast-paced.	Drug and alcohol-related attendance problems. Suprvsr. thinks applicants better educated. Attitudes are poor (among temps)—cites how demanding job is.	TopPoint Products 75%	Prod. Wker.	Bend steel tubing on automated machines—may do some welding. Do some SPC—use calculator. Use calipers. OTJ training.	Workers know firm is doing poorly. A lot of alcohol problems. Poor motivation. No problem with hard skills—communicate well ("to excess"). Fear of going to school: do better in-house.
Trail 100%	Prep. Wker	Job takes one month to learn. Prepare vehicles for paint and repair. Some math, no reading. Attitude and teamwork most important.	Sees decline in work ethic. Wkers hired to be trained in repair often demoted into this position. Said to be "bottom of the barrel."	Flamebest 40%	Prep. Wker	Wants HS degree—workers must be able to read. Prefers mechanical ability. Provide OTJ training. Tries to work with people—does not fire wkers.	Workers lack technical skills and have attitude problems: notes his own son fits into this category.

Company	Job Title		
Sears Metals 90%	Entry prod.	Entry level welder: rack repair. Described as dirty job. Few required skills: just ability to count and read.	Pres. sees deterioration in work ethic; supervisor sees opposite. Latter sees improvement in hard skills and work attitudes among young black workers.
Gratiot Welding 9%	Prod. Wker.	Rack repair and fabrication. Puts applicants through a welding test, but will train those with no experience.	Workers do not have problems with hard or soft skills because of "screening." Thinks people want to work harder than in the past.
Satellite Fast. 33%	Setup Trainee	Would like mechanical ability and experience. Need to read blueprints and use calipers. Need "common sense and reasoning ability." HS degree required.	Big decline in applicants with mechan. ability. No place for young people to learn such skills in Detroit. Has hired whites with skills to train blacks. Young workers don't want to work hard.
Planet Products 50%	Platg. Mach. Oper.	Some tech. changes in past 10 years—no change in requiremts. for job. Would like some mech. ability. Workers need some math; if they are to advance, should have some knowledge of chemistry. SPC done by computer.	Half of the applicants fail drug screen. Still find good workers. Big "burn-out" rate; personal problems. Send wkers to communication college to learn SPC. Workers have less hard skills than in suburbs, but have better work ethics.

Table C-1. Sample Job and Worker Skill Characteristics (*cont.*)

Bl. Firm/% Black	Samp. Job	Req. Skills	Worker Char.	Wh. Firm/% Black	Samp. Job	Req. Skills	Worker Char.
Morgan Stamp 87%	Press Oper.	Stamp metal parts. Automated press—do quality checking: SPC. President says work ethic most important. Supervisr. says takes 30 days to learn job; need 9th gr. math: observation skills.	Shifting more to women and older workers. Overall, applicants seen as having more skills than in the past. See more displaced workers and applicants with training.	**Dartmo. 35%**	Press Oper.	Stamp and assemble metal parts. Do quality checks, but have separate quality control that uses SPC. Key req.: observation skills.	Workers are "intelligent but poorly educated." Poor communication skills. No motivation. Resp. see this as wage effect. Applicants have more skills than in the past.
Silver Inc. 72%	Packer	Visually inspect parts. Check invoices and pack. One week to learn.	Black wkers self-conscious—confidence an issue. Good effort but poor work skills.	**Sargeant Gum 50%**	Packer	Check labels and invoices. Must be able to read: basic math. OTJ training.	Poor skills among applicants. No loyalty to firm. Math problems (city and suburb). 85-90% "success rate" after training.

CalOra. 100%	Mach. Oper.	Some manual operation: mostly automated. Formal training. Basic math, literacy imp. Tech skills taught OTJ.	Less good people coming through (after baby boom). Young people feels they are owed something. Poor prep. in basic skills fr. schools	**Armstrg. Industries 50%**	Prod. Worker	Cross-trained on a number of machines. Bending tubing. All automated. Repetitive. Heavy lifting. Ergonomic problems. Basic math for SPC.	Lots of applicants—many without high school degree. Supervisor says its a "good group"; feels poorer attitudes come with wage cuts.
Woodw. Gas No Info.	Fuel Plant Oper.	Fill propane cylinders—service customers on site. (no ladder). Stresses work skills: ethic and attitude. Must be literate; basic math.	Young wkers not serious. Poor work skills (not taught).	**USG 0%**	Fuel Distrib.	Fill cylinders on site. Can develop into route sales—go out to customer. Stresses good customer rapport. Heavy lifting. Need basic math and reading.	Workers unsatisfied with pay. Most applicants are HS grads; expected to get CDL. Most willing to work hard.

Table C-1. Sample Job and Worker Skill Characteristics (*cont.*)

Bl. Firm/% Black	Samp. Job	Req. Skills	Worker Char.	Wh. Firm/% Black	Samp. Job	Req. Skills	Worker Char.
Eliza. Plastic Prod. 65%	Mach. Operator	Workers cross-trained. Req. skills unchang. 6th grade math. Read instructional sheets. More automation has made job safer and easier.	No perceived racial differences in hard skills; half flunk math test (bit higher percentage among blacks). Older wkers have attitude prob. Ynger are slower.	**Mushrm. 5%**	Mach. Oper. (plastics)	Modular production; automated processes. Have formal training. Will teach all req. skills (except literacy). Require more teamwork.	Wkers weak communicators. Young people have poor attitudes. Many hs. dropouts among workers; some illiterate workers lack motivation.
Lionel 35%	Mach. Oper.	Production wkers—semiautomated machine. Demolds parts and trims—inspects. Use SPC. More autonomy. Need basic math. More communication skills.	Most difficult to train workers in color inspection. Workforce more educated overall "but lazy." More displaced wkers in pool. Young have poor attitudes.	**Janis Snap 0%**	Mach. Oper.	Use measuring devices: OTJ training for this. Machines run fast—must keep up. Inspect parts—use SPC.	one-tenth make it through probation—motivation problem. Alcohol a problem. Hard to find people with skills—"adapted" thru OTJ training. Problems with work ethic.

Twain Plastics 88%	Mach. Oper.	Pull parts off automated molding machines, trim and inspect. Pack parts. Do some assembly and mainten. "Easy" to learn. Need basic math and literacy. SPC.	Poor skills— hard to teach SPC. Attitudes very poor: some come in after displacement fr. higher-paying jobs. Chooses to hire "unemployables"	
Mash Inc. 3%	Mach. Oper.	Metal stamping; fashion parts from steel coil. Automated process. "Watch machine run"—make sure parts go into container. Need more commic. skills. Basic math and reading. Takes a few wks. to learn. Visual inspection of parts. some meas.—SPC		"Real deficiencies in math and reading." Keep one-tenth. Problems with wker. logic and reasoning. Wkers. too passive. No change in work ethic (good and bad).

Bibliography

Acs, Gregory, and Sheldon Danziger (1993). "Educational Attainment, Industrial Structure, and Male Earnings through the 1980's." *Journal of Human Resources* 28, Summer: 618-648.

Arkeny, R. (1997, September 1-7). "Archer Seeks $50M to Raze Buildings." *Crains Detroit Business*, 1, 19.

Baron, James N., and Andrew E. Newman (1990). "For What It's Worth: Organizations, Occupations, and the Value of Work Done by Women and Non-Whites." *American Sociological Review* 55:155-175.

Bates, Timothy, and Constance R. Dunham (1993). "Facilitating Upward Mobility Through Small Business Ownership," in *Urban Labor Markets and Job Opportunity*, ed. George E. Peterson and Wayne Vroman, Washington D.C.: Urban Institute Press.

Bendick, Marc, Charles W. Jackson, and Victor A. Reinoso (1993). "Measuring Employment Discrimination Through Controlled Experiments." Mimeo: Fair Employment Council of Greater Washington, Inc.

Blank, Rebecca (1998). *It Takes a Nation : A New Agenda for Fighting Poverty.* Princeton: Princeton University Press.

Bluestone, Barry, and Bennett Harrison (1982). *The Deindustrialization of America*. New York: Basic Books.

Bound, John, and Richard B. Freeman (1992). "What Went Wrong? The Erosion of the Relative Earnings and Employment of Young Black Men in the 1980's." *Quarterly Journal of Economics* 107: 201-232.

Bound, John, and Harry Holzer (1991). "Industrial Shifts, Skill Levels, and the Labor Market for White and Black Males." Mimeo: University of Michigan.

Cappelli, Peter (1993). "Are Skill Requirements Rising? Evidence from Production and Clerical Jobs." *Industrial and Labor Relations Review* 46, 3, 515-530.

——— (1996). "Technology and Skill Requirements: Implications for Eestablishment wage Structure," *Earnings Inequality, Special Issue of the New England Economic Review,* May/June: 139-54.

Carmines, Edward, and Richard Champagne, Jr. (1990). "The Changing Content of American Racial Attitudes: A Fifty Year Portrait." *Research in Micropolitics* 3: 187-208.

Carnoy, Martin (1994). *Faded Dreams, the Politics and Economics of Race in America.* Cambridge, England: Cambridge University Press.

Clark, W.A.V. (1988). "Understanding Residential Segregation in American Cities: Interpreting the Evidence." *Population Research and Policy Review* 7: 113-121.

Corcoran, Mary, and Sharon Parrott (1992). "Black Women's Economic Progress." Paper presented at the Social Science Research Council Conference on "The Urban Underclass: Perspectives from the Social Sciences." Ann Arbor, Mich., June 8-10.

Culp, Jerome, and Bruce H. Dunson (1986). "Brothers of a Different Color: A Preliminary Look at Treatment of Black and White Youth." In *The Black Youth Employment Crisis*, ed. Richard B. Freeman and Harry J. Holzer. Chicago: The University of Chicago Press.

Cutler, David M., and Edward L. Glaeser (1995). *Are Ghettos Good or Bad?* Working paper No. 5163, National Bureau of Economic Research. Cambridge, Mass.

Danziger, Sheldon, and Peter Gottschalk (1995). *America Unequal.* Cambridge, Mass. Harvard University Press.

Darden, Joe T. (1987). "Status of Urban Blacks 25 Years After the Civil Rights Act of 1964." *Sociology and Social Research* 73, 4: 1-13.

Darden, Joe T., and Richard Child Hill et al. (1987). *Detroit: Race and Uneven Development.* Philadelphia: Temple University Press.

Darity, William A. Jr. and Patrick L. Mason (1998). "Evidence on Discrimination in Employment: Codes of Color, Codes of Gender." *Journal of Economic Perspectives* 12, 2, Spring: 63-90.

Denton, Nancy A., and Douglas S. Massey (1988). "Residential Segregation of Blacks, Hispanics, and Asians by Socioeconomic Status and Generation." *Social Sciences Quarterly* 69: 797-817.

Doeringer, Peter B., et al. (1991). *Turbulence in the American Workplace.* New York and Oxford: Oxford University Press.

Dovidio, John, and Samuel Gaertner (1981). "The Effects of Race, Status, and Ability on Helping Behavior." *Social Psychology Quarterly* 44: 192-203

Economic Report of the President (ERP) (1998). Washington, D.C.

Ellwood, David T. (1982). "Teenage Unemployment: Permanent Scars or Temporary Blemishes?" In *The Youth Labor Market Problem: Its Nature, Causes and Consequences*, ed. Richard Freeman and David Wise. Chicago: The University of Chicago Press.

—— (1986): "The Spatial Mismatch Hypothesis: Are There Teenage Jobs Missing in the Ghetto?" In *The Black Youth Employment Crisis*, ed. Richard B. Freeman and Harry J. Holzer. Chicago: The University of Chicago Press.

England, Paula (1992). *Comparable Worth. Theories and Evidence*. New York: Aldine de Gruyter.

Fainstein, Norman (1986-1987). "The Underclass/Mismatch Hypothesis as an Explanation for Black Economic Deprivation." *Politics and Society* 15: 403-451.

Farley, Reynolds, Charlotte Steeh, and Maria Krysan (1994). "Stereotypes and Segregation: Neighborhoods in the Detroit Area." *The American Journal of Sociology* 100, 3: 750-780.

Farley, Reynolds et al. (1979). "Barriers to the Racial Integration of Neighborhoods: The Detroit Case." *The Annals of the American Academy of Political and Social Science* 441: 97-113.

Farley, Reynolds (1989). "Blacks and Whites: Narrowing the Gap?" *The Social World of Adolescents: International Perspectives*, ed. Klaus and Engel. Berlin and New York: W. de Gruyter.

Feagin, Joe (1991). "The Continuing Significance of Race: Antiblack Discrimination in Public Places," *American Sociological Review* 56: 101-116.

Ferguson, Ronald (1993). "New Evidence on the Growing Value of Skill and Consequences for Racial Disparity and Returns to Schooling." Paper H-93-10, Malcolm Wiener Center for Social Policy, John F. Kennedy School of Government, Harvard University.

—— (1995). "Shifting Challenges: Fifty Years of Economic Change Toward Black/White Earnings Inequality." *Daedulus* 124: 37-76.

Ferguson, Ronald, and Randall Filer (1986). "Do Better Jobs Make Better Workers? Absenteeism from Work Among Inner-City Black Youths." *The Black Youth Employment Crisis*, ed. Richard B. Freeman and Harry J. Holzer. Chicago: The University of Chicago Press.

Fernandez, Roberto (1991): "Race, Space, and Job Accessibility: Evidence from a Plant Relocation." Mimeo: Northwestern University.

—— (1992). "A Review of 'Why Black Men are Doing Worse in the Labor Market.'" Mimeo: for presentation at a conference on "The Urban Underclass: Perspectives from the Social Sciences" at the University of Michigan.

—— (1993). "Effects of Spatial and Skills Mismatches on Minority Employment." Proposal submitted to the Russell Sage Foundation.

Fix, Michael, and Raymond J. Struyk (1993). "Clear and Convincing Evidence: Measurement of Discrimination in America." Washington, D.C.: Urban Institute Press.

Flynn, David S., and David E. Cole (1988). "The U.S. Automotive Industry: Technology and Competitiveness." In *Is New Technology Enough? Making and Remaking Basic Industries*, ed. Donald A. Hicks. American Enterprise Institute for Public Policy Research. Lanham: University Press of America.

Fortin, Nicole M., and Thomas Lemieux (1997). "Institutional Changes and Rising Wage Inequality: Is There a Linkage?" *Journal of Economic Perspectives* 11, 2, Spring 1997: 21-40.

Freeman, Richard B. (1989). "Help Wanted: Disadvantaged Youths in a Labor Shortage Economy." National Bureau of Economic Research. April.

—— (1991). "Crime and the Economic Status of Disadvantaged Young Men," Mimeo for presentation at the Conference on Urban Labor Markets.

Freeman, Richard B., and David G. Branchflower (1992). "Unionism in the United States and Other OECD Countries." *Industrial Relations* 31, Winter: 56-79.

Frey, William H (1984). "Lifecourse Migration of Metropolitan Whites and Blacks and the Structure of Demographic Change in Large Central Cities." *American Sociological Review* 49, 6, December: 803-827.

Galster, George (1988). "Residential Segregation in American Cities: A Contrary Review." *Population Research and Policy Review* 7: 93-112.

Gittleman, Maury B., and David R. Howell (1992). "Job Quality, Labor Market Segmentation, and Earnings Inequality: Effects of Economic Restructuring in the 1980's by Race and Gender." Mimeo, Department of Economics, New York University, and Graduate School of Management, New School for Social Research. July.

Gordon, David (1972). *Theories of Poverty and Underemployment*. Lexington, Mass.: D.C. Heath.

Gordon, David, Richard Edwards, and Michael Reich (1982). *Segmented Work, Divided Workers: The Historical Transformations of Labor in the United States*. New York: Cambridge University Press.

Gottschalk, Peter (1997). "Inequality, Income Growth, and Mobility: The Basic Facts." *Journal of Economic Perspectives* 11, 2, Spring 1997: 21-40.

Granovetter, Mark (1974). *Getting an Job: A Study of Contacts and Careers.* Cambridge, Mass: Harvard University Press.

———— (1988). "The Sociological and Economic Approaches to Labor Markets" in *Industries, Firms, and Jobs: Sociological and Economic Approaches*, ed. George Farkas and Paula England. New York: Plenum.

Groshen, Erica, and R. Williams, Jr. (1991). "Five Reasons Why Wages Vary Among Employers." *Industrial Relations* 30, Fall: 350-381.

Hayghe, Howard (1997). "Development in Women's Labor Force Participation." Monthly Labor Review 120(9): 41-47.

Heckman, James, and Peter Siegelman (1991). "An Evaluation of the Methods and Findings of the Urban Insititute Employment Audit Studies." Mimeo prepared for the conference "Testing for Discrimination in America: Results and Policy Implications." Washington, D.C.

Heinlein, George (1995). "Detroit's Burglaries Down 4.1%, Report Says." *The Detroit News*, September 13.

Heinlein, George, and Carol Phillips (1996). "Detroit Crime Rate Declines." *The Detroit News*, May 6.

Hirsch, Barry T., and David A. Macpherson (1993). "Union Membership and Coverage Files from the Current Population Surveys." *Industrial and Labor Relations Review* 46(3), April 1993: 574-78.

Hirsch, Barry T., and Edward J. Schumacher (1992). "Labor Earnings, Discrimination, and the Racial Composition of Jobs." *Journal of Human Resources* 27: 602-628.

Holzer, Harry (1987). "Informal Job Search and Black Youth Unemployment." *American Economic Review* 77: 446-452.

———— (1991). "The Spatial Mismatch Hypothesis: What Has the Evidence Shown?" *Urban Studies* 28, 105-122.

———— (1995). "Employer Hiring Decisions and Antidiscrimination Policy." Working Paper #86. New York, N.Y.: Russell Sage Foundation.

———— (1996). "What Employers Want: Job Prospects for the Less Educated." New York: Russell Sage Foundation Press.

Holzer, Harry, and Keith Ihlanfeldt (1995). "Spatial Factors and the Employment of Blacks at the Firm Level." Paper prepared for the Symposium on Spatial and Labor Market Contributions to Earnings Inequality, Federal Reserve Bank of Boston. Boston, Mass.

Holzer, Harry, Keith Ihlanfeldt, and David L. Sjoquist (1992). "Work, Search, and Travel among White and Black Youth." Paper prepared for the 1992 TRED Conference on Inner City Poverty and Unemployment. New York, N.Y.

Holzer, Harry, and Richard Freeman (1989). "Young Blacks and Jobs." In *Labor Markets in Action: Essays in Empirical Economics*. Cambridge: Harvard University Press: 121-133.

Howell, David, and Edward Wolff (1991). "Trends in the Growth and Distribution of Skills in the U.S. Workplace, 1960-1985." *Industrial and Labor Relations Review* 44, 3, 481-501.

Hughes, Mark, and Janice Fanning Madden (1991). Residential Segregation and the Economic Status of Black Workers: New Evidence for an Old Debate." *Journal of Urban Economics* 29 (1), 28-49.

Ihlanfeldt, Keith R. (1989). "The Impact of Job Decentralization on the Economic Welfare of Central-City Blacks." *Journal of Urban Economics* 26 (July): 110-130.

————— (1997). "The Geography of Economic and Social Opportunity within Metropolitan Areas." Prepared for the Committee on Improving the Future of U.S. Cities Through Improved Metropolitan Governance, National Council/National Academy of Science. February.

Ihlanfeldt, Keith. R., and D.L. Sjoquist (1990). "Job Accessibility and Racial Differences in Youth Employment Rates." *American Economic Review* 80: 267-276.

Jackson, Kenneth (1985). *The Crabgrass Frontier*. New York: Oxford University Press.

Jaynes, G. and Williams, R. Jr., eds. (1989). *A Common Destiny: Blacks and American Society*. Washington D.C.: Washington National Academy Press.

Jencks, Christopher, and Susan E. Mayer (1989). "Residential Segregation, Job Proximity, and Black Job Opportunities: The Empirical Status of the Spatial Mismatch Hypothesis." Mimeo, Northwestern University.

————— (1991). "Is the American Underclass Growing?" In *The Urban Underclass*, ed. Christopher Jencks and Paul E. Peterson. Washington D.C.: The Brookings Institution.

Johnson, James H. Jr., and Melvin Oliver (1990). "Economic Restructuring and Black Male Joblessness in U.S. Metropolitan Areas." Mimeo: Center for the Study of Urban Poverty, University of California, Los Angeles.

Juhn, Chinhui (1999). "Wage Inequality and Demand for Skill: Evidence from Five Decades." *Industrial and Labor Relations Review* 52 (3), April: 424-443.

————— (1992). "The Decline of Male Labor Market Participation: the Role of Declining Market Opportunities." *The Quarterly Journal of Economics* 187, February: 79-121.

Kain, John (1968). "Housing Segregation, Negro Employment and Metropolitan Decentralization." *Quarterly Journal of Economics*. May.

Kasarda, John D. (1988). "Urban Change and Minority Opportunities," in Paul E. Peterson, ed., *The New Urban Reality*. Washington D.C.: National Academy Press.

Katz, Lawrence, and Kevin Murphy (1992). "Changes in Relative Wages, 1963-1987: Supply and Demand Factors." *Quarterly Journal of Economics* 107: 35-78.

Kaufman, Robert L. (1986). "The Impact of Industrial and Occupational Structure on Black-White Employment Allocations." *American Sociological Review* 51 June: 310-323.

Keefe, Jeffrey H. (1992). "Do Unions HInder Technological Change?" In Lawrence Michel and Paula B. Voos, ed., *Unions and Economic Competitiveness*. London: Sharpe: 109-142.

Kirschenman, Joleen, and Katherine Neckerman (1991a). "Hiring Strategies, Racial Bias and Inner-City Workers." *Social Problems* 38: 433-447.

—— (1991b). " ' We'd Love to Hire Them, But . . . ': the Meaning of Race for Employers" in *The Urban Underclass*, edited by Christopher Jencks and Paul E. Peterson, Washington D.C.: The Brookings Institution.

—— (1991c). "Chicago Employer Survey." Notes from Methodology.

Kutscher, Donald E., and Valerie A. Personick (1986). "Deindustrialization and the Shift to Services." *Monthly Labor Review* June: 3-15

Leonard, Jonathan S. (1987). "The Interaction of Residential Segregation and Employment Discrimination." *Journal of Urban Economics* 21: 323-346.

—— (1990). "The Impact of Affirmative Action Regulation and Equal Opportunity Law on Black Employment." *Journal of Economic Perspectives* 4, Fall: 47-63.

Levy, Frank, and Richard Murnane (1992). "U.S. Earnings Levels and Earnings Inequality: A Review of Recent Trends and Proposed Explanations." *Journal of Economic Literature* 30, 3: 1333-1381.

Levy, Frank, Richard J. Murnane, and Lijian Chen (1993). "Where We Are: The Impact of Recent Restructuring on Jobs and Earnings." Mimeo: Harvard Graduate School of Education and MIT Department of Urban Studies.

Lieberson, Stanley (1980). *A Piece of the Pie*. Berkeley: University of California Press.

Logan, John R., and Mark Schneider (1982). "Suburban Racial Segregation and Black Access to Local Public Resources." *Social Science Quarterly* 63(4): 762-778.

Mare, Robert D., and Christopher Winship (1984). "The Paradox of Lessening Racial Inequality and Joblessness Among Black Youth: Enrollment, Enlistment, and Employment, 1964-1981." *American Sociological Review* 49, February: 39-55.

Marx, Jonathan (1992). "Formality of Recruitment to 229 Jobs." *Sociology and Social Research* 76: 190-196.

Massey, Douglas S. (1990). "American Apartheid: Segregation and the Making of the Underclass." *American Journal of Sociology* 96: 329-357.

Massey, Douglas S., et al. (1987). "The Effect of Residential Segregation on Black Economic Well-Being." *Social Forces* 66: 29-56.

Massey, Douglas S., and Nancy A. Denton (1988). "Suburbanization and Segregation in U.S. Metropolitan Areas." *American Journal of Sociology* 94, 3 November: 592-626.

———— (1989). "Hypersegregation in U.S. Metropolitan Areas: Black and Hispanic Segregation Along Five Dimensions." *Demography* 26 (3): August: 373-391.

Mayer, Susan, and Christopher Jencks (1989). "Growing Up in Poor Neighborhoods, How Much Does it Matter?" *Science* 243: March 17, 1441-1445.

McIntosh, Neil, and David J. Smith (1974). "The Extent of Racial Discrimination," Broadsheet 40 (547). London: PEP, The Social Science Institute.

Mead, Lawrence M. (1989). "The Logic of Workfare: The Underclass and Work Policy." In *The Annals of the American Academy of Political Science,* ed. William Julius Wilson, Vol. 501. Newbury Park, London, New Delhi: Sage Publications.

Mincy, Ronald B. (1991). "The Urban Institute Audit Studies: Their Research and Policy Context." Mimeo prepared for the conference "Testing for Discrimination in America: Results and Policy Implications." Washington, D.C.

Mishel, Lawrence, and Ruy A. Teixeira (1990). *The Myth of the Coming Labor Shortage: Jobs, Skills, and Incomes of America's Workforce 2000.* Washington, D.C.: Economic Policy Institute.

Moss, Phillip, and Chris Tilly (1991a). "Why Black Men are Doing Worse in the Labor Market: A Review of Supply-Side and Demand-Side Explanations." Social Science Research Council. Washington, D.C.

———— (1991b). "Raised Hurdles for Black Men: Evidence from Interviews with Employers." Paper presented at the annual meeting of the Association for Public Policy Analysis and Management. Bethesda, Maryland. October 24.

———— (1994). Unpublished interview data from research project entitled: "Why Aren't Employers Hiring More Black Men?"

———— (1996). "Soft Skills and Race: An Investigation of Black Men's Employment Problems." *Work and Occupations* 23, 3: 252-276.

———— (1998). "Hiring in Urban Labor Markets: Shifting Labor Demands, Persistent Racial Differences." *Sourcebook on Labor Markets, Evolving Structures and Processes,* ed. Ivar Berg and Arne Kallegerg. Unpublished manuscript.

Murnane, Richard J. (1992). "Restructuring Work and Learning," in *Urban Labor Markets and Job Opportunity*, ed. George Peterson and Wayne Vroman. Washington D.C.: Urban Institute Press.

Murnane, Richard J., and Frank Levy (1994) "Skills, Demography and the Economy: Is There a Mismatch?" In *Labor Markets, Employment Policy and Job Creation*, ed. Lewis C. Solmon and Alec R. Levenson. Milkin Institute Series in Economics and Education. Boulder: Westview Press: 361-376.

———— (1996). *Teaching the New Basic Skills*. New York: The Free Press.

Neal, Derek A., and William R. Johnson (1996). "The Role of Premarket Factors in Black-White Wage Differences." *Journal of Political Economy* 104, 5, October: 869-895.

Neill, William J.V. (1995). "Lipstick on the Gorilla: the Failure of Image-led Planning in Coleman Young's Detroit." *International Journal of Urban and Regional Planning* 19: 639-653.

Newman, Katherine, and Carol B. Stack (1992). "Why Work? The Meaning of Labor and Sources of Dignity in Minority Adolescent Lives." Unpublished manuscript.

Noyelle, Thierry (1987). *Beyond Industrial Dualism*. Boulder, Colo.: Westview Press.

O'Neill, June (1990). "The Role of Human Capital in Earnings Differences Between Black and White Men." *The Journal of Economic Perspectives* 4, 25-46.

Olson, Walter (1992). *The Litigation Explosion*. New York: Truman Talley Books.

Orfield, Gary (1992). "Urban Schooling and the Perpetuation of Job Inequality in Metropolitan Chicago." In *Urban Labor Markets and Job Opportunity*, ed. Peterson and Vroman. Washington D.C.: Urban Institute Press.

Osterman, Paul (1975). "An Empirical Study of Labor Market Segmentation." *Industrial and Labor Relations Review*, July.

———— (1980). *Getting Started*. Cambridge: M.I.T. Press.

———— (1988). *Employment Futures: Reorganization, Dislocation, and Public Policy*. New York: Oxford University Press.

———— (1995). "Skill, Training and Work Organization in American Establishments." *Industrial Relations* 34, 2: 125-146.

Parmar, Pratibha (1982). "Gender, Race and Class: Asian Women in Resistance." *The Empire Strikes Back: Race and Racism in 70s Britain*. University of Birmingham: Hutchinson in Association with Center for Contemporary Studies.

Patton, Michael Quinn (1990). *Qualitative Evaluation and Research Methods*. Newbury Park, Calif.: Sage Publications.

Peterson, George E., and Wayne Vroman, eds. (1992). *Urban Labor Markets and Job Opportunity*. Washington D.C.: Urban Institute Press.

Pettigrew, Thomas, and Joanne Martin (1987). "Shaping the Organizational Context for Black American Inclusion." *Journal of Social Issues* 43: 41-78.

Rodgers, William M. III, and William Spriggs (1996). "What Does the AFQT Really Measure: Race, Wages and Schooling and the AFQT Score." *Review of Black Political Economy*, 24, 4: 13-46.

Rosenbaum, James E., and Susan J. Popkin (1991). "Employment and Earnings of Low-Income Blacks Who Move to Middle-Class Suburbs." In *The Urban Underclass*, ed. Christopher Jencks and Paul E. Peterson. Washington D.C.: The Brookings Institute.

Rumberger, Russell, and Martin Carnoy (1980). "Segmentation in the U.S. Labor Market —Its Effect on the Mobility and Earnings of Blacks and Whites." *Cambridge Journal of Economics* 4: 117-132.

Siegelman, Peter, and Ian Ayres (1991). "Using Audits to Test for Discrimination in Hiring: An Economic Analysis." Mimeo prepared for the conference "Testing for Discrimination in America: Results and Policy Implications."

Smith, James P., and Finish Welch (1984). "Affirmative Action and Labor Markets." *Journal of Labor Economics*, 2, 2: 269-301.

Southeast Metropolitan Council of Governments (SEMCOG) (1991). "Social Impacts: Crime, Race, Education 1990-2010." Regional Development Briefing Paper #2. Detroit, Mich.

Spenner, Kenneth I. (1995). "Technological Change, Skill Requirements, and Education: The Case for Uncertainty." *The New Modern Times: Factors Reshaping the World of Work*, ed. David B. Bills. Albany: State University of New York Press: 81-137.

Sullivan, Mercer (1989). *"Getting Paid": Youth Crime and Work in the Inner-City*. Ithaca, N.Y.: Cornell University Press.

Sum, Andrew M., Paul E. Harrington, and William C. Goedicke (1987). "One Fifth of the Nation's Teenagers: Employment Problems of Youth in America, 1981-85." *Youth and Society* 18, 3: 195-257.

Turner, Margery, and Michael Fix (1991). "Opportunities Denied, Opportunities Diminished: Discrimination in Hiring." Mimeo: The Urban Institute.

Turner, Susan (1993). "Henry Ford and the Black Men of Detroit." Paper presented at the Association of the Collegiate Schools of Planning. Tuscon, Ariz.

——— (1997). "Barriers to a Better Break: Employer Discrimination and Spatial Mismatch in Metropolitan Detroit." *Journal of Urban Affairs* 19, 2: 123-141.

Turner Meiklejohn, Susan (1999). "Has Discrimination Disappeared? A Reply to W. J. Wilson on Black Workers and 'Soft' Skills." *Economic Development Quarterly* 13, November.

———— (1998). "Zone Is Where the Heart Is?: Lessons from Detroit Employers." *Economic Development Quarterly* 12, November.

Vroman, Wayne, and George E. Peterson (1992). Urban Labor Markets and Job Opportunites. Washington D.C.: Urban Institute Press.

Waldinger, Roger (1986-1987). "Changing Ladders and Musical Chairs: Ethnicity and Opportunity in Post-Industrial New York." *Politics and Society* 15, 4: 369-401.

———— (1993). "Who Makes the Beds, Who Washes the Dishes?: Black/Immigrant Competition Reassessed." Working Paper 246. Institute of Industrial Relations, University of California at Los Angeles.

———— (1993b). *Still the Promised City?: African-Americans and New Immigrants in Postindustrial New York.* Cambridge, Mass: Harvard University Press, 1993.

Weis, Lois (1990). *Working Class Without Work: High School Students in a Deindustrializing Economy.* New York: Routledge.

Welch, Finis (1990). "The Employment of Black Men." *Journal of Labor Economics,* 8, 1, Pt. 2, January: S26-S74.

Willis, Paul (1977). *Learning to Labor: How Working Class Kids Get Working Class Jobs.* New York: Columbia University Press.

Wilson, William Julius (1987). *The Truly Disadvantaged.* Chicago: The University of Chicago Press.

———— (1996). *When Work Disappears: The World of the New Urban Poor.* New York: Alfred A. Knopf.

Word, C.O., M.P. Zanna, and J. Cooper (1974). "The Nonverbal Mediation of Self-Fulfilling Prophecies in Interracial Interaction." *Journal of Experimental Social Psychology* 10: 100-120 .

Yin, Robert K. (1989). *Case Study Research: Design and Methods.* Newbury Park, Calif.: Sage Publications.

Zax, Jeffrey S., and John Kain (1991). "The Substitution Between Moves and Quits." *The Economic Journal* 101, November: 1510-1521.

Index